The 50 Days that Changed Europe

For Ruben and Thomas

If you don't know where you come from,
you don't know who you are.

The 50

Days that
Changed Europe

Hanneke Siebelink

LUSTER

Contents

Introduction   9

EU member states   10

1   *9 May 1950*
Schuman launches an ambitious plan   12

2   *18 April 1951*
Six countries sign the Treaty of Paris   14

3   *30 August 1954*
France votes no and sinks the European defence plan   16

4   *3 June 1955*
A new dawn for Europe   18

5   *25 March 1957*
The Six sign the Treaties of Rome   20

6   *14 January 1962*
The common agricultural policy is agreed   22

7   *14 January 1963*
Charles De Gaulle slams the door on the British   24

8   *5 February 1963*
Van Gend & Loos: a milestone in European legal history   27

9   *1 July 1965*
The Empty Chair Crisis   29

10   *29 January 1966*
The Luxembourg Compromise   31

11   *2 December 1969*
A new spirit   33

1 January 1973
Europe gains three new members   35

23 April 1973
Kissinger declares 1973 'The Year of Europe'   37

10 December 1974
The European Council is created   40

7 June 1979
The European Parliament is elected by the voters   42

29 November 1979
Mrs Thatcher demands her money back   44

26 June 1984
The Fontainebleau Agreement   46

7 January 1985
Jacques Delors takes over the Commission   48

14 January 1985
Delors launches Project 1992   50

29 June 1985
Craxi pulls off a coup   52

17 February 1986
The Single European Act changes the Treaty of Rome   54

17 April 1989
A blueprint for economic and monetary union   56

7 October 1989
Gorbachev's kiss   58

9 November 1989
The Berlin Wall comes down   61

9 December 1989
Monetary union in return for German reunification   63

26   *3 October 1990*
Germany is reunited   65

27   *30 September 1991*
The Dutch back the wrong horse   67

28   *10 December 1991*
The European Union is born in Maastricht   69

29   *22 June 1993*
The door is open   72

30   *15 December 1993*
The Uruguay Round ends in success   74

31   *25 June 1994*
Who will succeed Jacques Delors?   76

32   *1 January 1995*
Austria, Sweden and Finland join the EU   78

33   *18 June 1997*
Small changes to the treaty at the Amsterdam Summit   80

34   *1 January 1999*
Economic and monetary union takes off   83

35   *15 December 2001*
The Laeken Declaration   85

36   *15 January 2003*
A deal is reached on a permanent president   87

37   *10 July 2003*
One step closer to a European constitution   89

38   *1 May 2004*
The big bang: from 15 to 25 member states in one day   92

39   *18 June 2004*
Blair blocks Verhofstadt as Commission president   94

21 September 2004
The Services Directive comes under fire96

29 May 2005
France kills off the European constitution99

1 January 2007
Romania and Bulgaria join the EU101

22 June 2007
Brussels Summit lays down the foundations for the Lisbon Treaty103

17 September 2007
European Commission versus Microsoft: 1 - 0105

13 December 2007
The Lisbon Treaty is signed108

23 January 2008
Barroso presents an ambitious plan on energy and climate change110

19 November 2009
Finally, the European Council has a permanent president112

10 February 2010
Barroso Commission II takes over115

6 May 2010
The European Parliament shows its teeth118

9 May 2010
The eurozone receives a massive bailout121

*Index*124

*Credits*128

With thanks to Jean-Luc Dehaene
for reading the text and for his valuable suggestions.

Introduction

Some 500 million people have joined together in a unique experiment called the European Union. This Union is now one of the world's great power blocs. It consists of 27 sovereign states, each with its own culture, history and local pride. These countries, led by their prime ministers and presidents, have worked together on a project that aims to increase their collective economic influence while strengthening the bonds of political cooperation. Achieving this goal is a complex process that doesn't always run smoothly. This is especially true now, in 2011, when the crisis engulfing the euro threatens the future of the Union. The links that have been forged over several decades are being put to the test as never before.

What are the forces that played a role in making this European Union? What are the events that have shaped it? Who are the people who helped to bring about these fundamental changes in Europe? What were their motives and how did they show their leadership? How did their decisions affect the lives of Europeans and what are the challenges that lie ahead for us?

In answer to these questions, this book presents the history of Europe in 50 episodes and images. It sets out to sketch a chronological account of the creation of the European Union, but, more importantly, to offer an insight into the people behind the most important moments in our history. These 50 stories take you, as it were, into the kitchen where the decisions are made – bringing you close to the reality that is often simply dismissed as 'Brussels'. This book sets out to narrow the gap between Brussels and the citizen. The European machine has a profound impact on our lives, and it is made up of people just like you and me.

Hanneke Siebelink

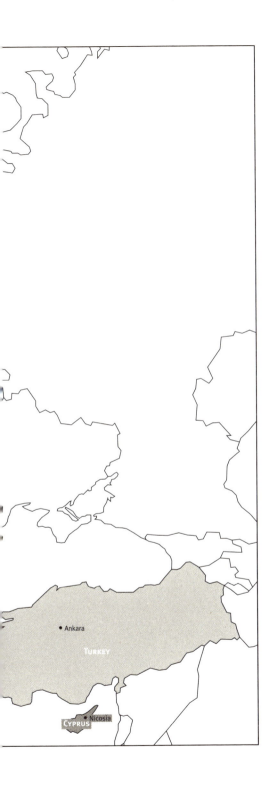

EU member states

1951	Six	Belgium
		The Netherlands
		Luxembourg
		Germany
		France
		Italy
1973	Nine	United Kingdom
		Ireland
		Denmark
1981	Ten	Greece
1986	Twelve	Spain
		Portugal
1995	Fifteen	Finland
		Sweden
		Austria
2004	Twenty-five	Czech Republic
		Slovakia
		Estonia
		Latvia
		Lithuania
		Hungary
		Slovenia
		Poland
		Malta
		Cyprus
2007	Twenty-seven	Bulgaria
		Romania

Candidate member states

(in 2011)	Turkey
	Croatia
	Iceland
	Former Yugoslav Republic of Macedonia
	Montenegro

1

9 May 1950

Schuman launches an ambitious plan

A white marble mantlepiece decorated with pious-looking angels. Enormous chandeliers hang from the ceiling, illuminating the room with a golden light, as if aware that the declaration that is about to be read would resonate through the ages. It was in this august setting – the Salon de l'Horloge in the French foreign ministry – that on May 9, 1950 foreign minister Robert Schuman put on his black glasses, cleared his throat, and addressed the expectant crowd of journalists.

'In taking upon herself for more than 20 years the role of champion of a united Europe,' he said in his shrill voice, 'France has always had as her essential aim the service of peace. A united Europe was not achieved and we had war.'

'Europe will not be made all at once, or according to a single plan. It will be built through concrete achievements which first create a de facto solidarity. The coming together of the nations of Europe requires the elimination of the age-old opposition of France and Germany. Any action taken must in the first place concern these two countries.'

'With this aim in view,' he continued, 'the French government proposes that action be taken immediately on one limited but decisive point. It proposes that Franco-German production of coal and steel as a whole be placed under a common High Authority, within the framework of an organization open to the participation of the other countries of Europe. [...] The solidarity in production thus established will make it plain that any war between France and Germany becomes not merely unthinkable, but materially impossible. [...] By pooling basic production and by instituting a new High Authority, whose decisions will bind France, Germany and other member countries, this proposal will lead to the realisation of the first concrete foundation of a European federation indispensable to the preservation of peace.'[1]

There was consternation in the room. Journalists, scribbling away madly, looked perplexed. Here and there, applause broke out. A supranational institution that could take binding decisions on behalf of France, Germany and other states? They were curious to see what Konrad Adenauer, the newly-elected Chancellor of postwar West Germany, would make of it all.

1   Robert Schuman, Declaration of 9 May 1950, Paris. The date 9 May is an official holiday for European institutions.

It quickly became clear that Adenauer was fully behind the proposal. For him, this presented an opportunity to lift his country out of the humiliating isolation it had suffered after the folly of World War Two. He had already given Schuman his support the night before the foreign minister launched his famous plan. Even the United States had encouraged France to take such a step. Now that the Cold War with Russia was turning more serious, it was more important than ever that West Germany was anchored in the free world.

Who was the architect of this ingenious plan that put Schuman in the media spotlight on May 9? It was in fact the work of the senior French diplomat Jean Monnet – a small man with a big vision. It is worth re-reading his memoires. 'It is not feelings of friendship that create a community,' he wrote, but, conversely, that working together creates friendship.' Monnet put people at the centre of the project. 'We are not binding states,' he said, 'We are uniting people.'[2]

2   Jean Monnet quoted in Geert Mak, *In Europe*, 2008, p. 625.

Photo:
Jean Monnet (left) and Robert Schuman during negotiations on the Schuman Plan

2

18 April 1951
Six countries sign the Treaty of Paris

Five countries listened to Schuman's appeal and sat down with France at the negotiating table. Germany, Italy, Belgium, the Netherlands and Luxembourg were all involved. The United Kingdom – by far the most powerful European country after the Second World War – failed to show up.

The British prime minister Clement Attlee was opposed to the High Authority, describing it as 'an irresponsible body appointed by no one and responsible to no one'. Perhaps he was angry with Schuman because he had read his declaration without briefing him in person.

The end result was that the negotiations around this new European construction began with a core group of six countries. The territory covered by the six countries roughly corresponded to the empire ruled by Charlemagne in the Middle Ages. In old manuscripts, Charlemagne is often referred to as the 'father of Europe'. He ruled at a time before the French and Germans were divided. The perfect symbol for Europe, you might say.

3   Max Kohnstamm, quoted in Geert Mak, *In Europe*, 2008, p. 625.

Most of the participants agreed that the negotiations were historic. 'The contacts were very personal,' according to the Dutch diplomat Max Kohnstamm, who served as Jean Monnet's right-hand man for many years. 'The mood was very different to the tough bilateral agreements that were the norm, particularly in the poor postwar years,' he told the Dutch writer Geert Mak in an interview published in In Europe. For us – the negotiators – it was a liberating experience. We were busy constructing structures that were entirely new. Everyone was aware of the fact that this went much further than simply the creation of a Coal and Steel Community involving a few European countries. There were open discussions that went beyond the immediate issues and didn't involve hidden agendas. There was a dynamic unlike anything before.'[3]

This was the moment when the European institutions were first shaped. The treaty that the six countries signed – known in full as the Treaty establishing the European Coal and Steel Community – made provision for a High Authority (the forerunner of the present Commission) which would make binding decisions in the 'general European interest', and a Court of Justice that would ensure that the provisions of the treaty were followed.

The Netherlands pushed for the creation of the Council of Ministers to include a role for national governments. Finally, a Common Assembly was established, consisting of national elected representatives but not yet officially known as a 'parliament'.

The aim of the treaty, according to the founding fathers, was to create 'an ever closer union among the peoples of Europe.'[4]

On 18 April 1951, six men in dark suits entered the Salon de l'Horloge in Paris. Robert Schuman, as host, was immensely proud. He was accompanied by the 75-year-old Konrad Adenauer, who was on his first official visit as Chancellor of West Germany, but was acting here as Germany's foreign minister. Also in attendance were Carlo Sforza for Italy, Paul Van Zeeland for Belgium, Dirk Stikker for the Netherlands and Joseph Bech representing Luxembourg. Watched by the foreign press, the ministers lined up to put their signature to the treaty, beginning with Adenauer representing *Allemagne*.

It was done. The Treaty of Paris was signed. Six European countries had surrendered a part of their sovereignty to a supranational organisation. It was the first time this had happened in Europe's history.

4   Treaty establishing the European Coal and Steel Community (ECSC), preamble.

Photo:
Robert Schuman and Konrad Adenauer sign the Treaty establishing the European Coal and Steel Community

3

30 August 1954

France votes no and sinks the European defence plan

For Jean Monnet, the intellect behind the Schuman Plan, the discussions about coal and steel were just the first step towards his vision of a united Europe. With the rise of the Communist threat, he believed that Europe needed a common institution in the field of defence, too, to withstand possible attacks. The idea had already taken shape in his mind: there would be agreements that an attack on one of the six member states would be considered as an attack on them all. The member states could keep a national army to protect their colonies and the head of state, but all other troops were to be put in the hands of the Community. There would be common institutions, just as was the case with coal and steel – a Commission, Council of Ministers, a Parliament and a Court of Justice. All of the soldiers would wear the same uniform.

It was just after the outbreak of the Korean War in 1950 when he approached his boss, the French prime minister René Pleven, with his proposal for the next great leap forward for Europe. It was accepted. Pleven threw his weight behind the plan and in October 1950 launched a call for 'the creation, in the interests of our common security, of a European army under the control of the political institutions of the united Europe.'

Monnet was an energetic networker. He talked to Eisenhower – who had just taken over as head of Nato – and convinced him of the importance of a European Defence Community. Eisenhower then persuaded Truman. Before Europe had really realised it, a far-reaching European defence treaty lay on the table. It contained all the provisions mentioned above.

The six members of the European Coal and Steel Community (ECSC) signed the treaty in May 1952. The United Kingdom was hostile to the plan and refused to sign. A European army made up of soldiers who didn't speak one another's language and couldn't understand the simplest order? Churchill found it a ridiculous idea.

The ECSC was officially launched at the end of 1952. The national parliaments had enthusiastically adopted the Treaty of Paris. Monnet was the first president of the High Authority. He had a broad smile on his face as he opened his new office in Luxembourg. Max Kohnstamm was his secretary. 'It was hard work,' Kohnstamm said, looking back on that period. 'Monnet was exceptionally inspiring, but, to put it mildly, he did not put a great deal of emphasis on hierarchy and bureaucratic structures. I can remember him coming into the office after a decision had finally been hammered out and saying: 'The High Authority has to meet again to consider the issue. Last night, my driver said something that we have to think about. Because he was right.'[5]

The Council assembled for the first time in full glory in September 1952. It was big news in Europe and across the world. The first decision that the six ministers took could not have been more clear. In preparation for the ratification of the defence treaty, they decided to work on a draft treaty for a 'European Political Community'. Their reasoning was that you could not have a good army without a unified political structure. Monnet and his federalist friends – including the Belgian foreign minister Paul-Henri Spaak – had every reason to congratulate themselves. Their dream of a free and united Western Europe was rapidly becoming a reality.

But the illusion was shattered on 30 August 1954. The French parliament had voted against the European defence treaty. Countless books have been written to explain the decision. The pro-European Christian Democrat party of Schuman and Pleven was no longer in the French government. Stalin had just died. And the mere thought of Germans in uniform again was enough to get the French running for cover.

The absence of the United Kingdom was another worry. An economic community without Britain was not such a big problem, but an army without the UK's participation was a different matter altogether.
This was a huge blow for Monnet. His own country had vetoed plans for a European Defence Community, along with plans for a political union. West Germany was incorporated into Nato's military structure and France, at least for the time being, was no longer the leading country in the creation of a united Europe.

5   Max Kohnstamm, quoted in Geert Mak, *In Europe*, 2008, p. 626.

4

3 June 1955
A new dawn for Europe

Maybe it was the result of the summer heatwave. On 3 June, 1955, less than a year after the failed attempt to set up a European Defence Community, the foreign ministers of the six ECSC member states reached an agreement in the Sicilian city of Messina.

'The Governments of the German Federal Republic, Belgium, France, Italy, Luxembourg and the Netherlands believe the moment has come to go a step further towards the construction of Europe,' the Declaration said. 'In their opinion this step should first of all be taken in the economic field. They consider that the further progress must be towards the setting up of a united Europe by the development of common institutions, the gradual merging of national economies, the creation of a common market, and the gradual harmonization of their social policies. Such a policy appears to them to be indispensable if Europe's position in the world is to be maintained, her influence restored, and the standard of living of her population progressively raised.'[6]

In fact, the ministers discussed two different plans while they were in Messina. The first came from Jean Monnet, who was now focusing his mind on a new area of action for the ECSC: nuclear power, the energy source of the future.

The second plan was put forward by the Dutch foreign minister Johan Willem Beyen, who had never genuinely believed in political unification without economic integration, and who had now dusted off an earlier plan for a European market. The ministers meeting in Messina decided that both plans – a nuclear cartel and a common market – offered a way forwards. And they went even further and asked a committee of experts to draw up a feasibility plan for each of these projects.

Paul-Henri Spaak, the Belgian minister of foreign affairs, was unanimously elected to chair this committee. No wonder photographs from this period show Spaak looking very pleased with himself under the hot Sicilian sun, as if he had always known that he would be the man to shape Europe.

Spaak reached his conclusions within a year. The Spaak report argued for the creation of a European Atomic Energy Community, which would stimulate pioneering research into the peaceful use of nuclear energy. As for the European market, Spaak argued for nothing less than a complete customs

6   Declaration of Messina, 3 June 1955.

union. This customs union would require the creation of a common tariff with regard to the outside world, in contrast to a free trade area, where the participating countries eliminate internal trade restrictions (tariffs, quantitative restrictions), but maintain their own external tariffs. The implementation of a common external tariff is a much more significant step, leading to a common trade policy and a unified stance by the Community towards the outside world.

The Benelux countries and Italy were in favour of this level of integration, since their economies had everything to gain from such a policy. France was more reluctant and Germany was initially divided. The British, who had been invited to take part in the discussions, were sceptical about the success of the treaty: 'The future treaty which you are discussing has no chance of being agreed; if it was agreed, it would have no chance of being ratified; and if it was ratified, it would have no chance of being applied. And if it was applied, it would be totally unacceptable to Britain. You speak of agriculture, which we don't like, of power over customs, which we take exception to, and of institutions, which frighten us. Monsieur le president, messieurs, au revoir et bonne chance'.[7]

7   Quoted in Charles Grant, *Delors*, 1994, p. 62.

Exit the British. The six countries that remained at the table did not take this to heart. They decided to follow Spaak's recommendations and to begin formal negotiations. The negotiations were conducted in the Château de Val Duchesse (Kasteel Hertoginnedal in Dutch), in the leafy suburbs of Brussels. This beautiful aristocratic retreat has an important place in history. The ministers and diplomats who entered the gates came out again with a historic agreement.

Photo:
The foreign ministers of Germany, France, Italy, Belgium, the Netherlands and Luxembourg gather in Messina

5

25 March 1957

The Six sign the Treaties of Rome

There is no denying that Spaak, as chairman, played a leading role in steering the negotiations towards their conclusion. When the going got tough, Adenauer stepped in to assist with a mixture of leadership and generosity. The basic terms of the agreement signed by the Six in 1957 to set up the European Economic Community can be summarised briefly.

- The abolition of customs duties and quotas on imports and exports between the member states over a period of 12 years.
- The introduction of a common external tariff and a common trade policy, which laid the basis for the job currently held by Karel De Gucht, European Commissioner for Trade.
- Free movement of people, services and capital between the member states.
- The introduction of a common agricultural policy, a demand introduced by France in the closing stages of the negotiations.
- A guarantee of fair competition in the common market. This ultimately led to the creation of the post of European Commissioner for Competition, a role skillfully performed by people such as Sir Leon Brittan, Peter Sutherland, Karel Van Miert and Neelie Kroes.

8   Treaty establishing the European Economic Community, preamble.

At this stage, the negotiations avoided consideration of lofty political goals. The Six were, however, determined that the integration of their markets would in time lead to an 'ever closer union between the people of Europe'.[8]

The second agreement set up Euratom, the European Atomic Energy Community. This was designed to encourage research, disseminate knowledge and generate investment to create a powerful nuclear energy sector in Europe.

The institutions which were created six years earlier remained in existence. The only change was that the member states gave themselves the power to legislate, rather than the High Authority, or, as it was subsequently named, the Commission.

The Commission was given the exclusive right to propose European legislation. The Council of Minister would then reach decisions on the basis of the proposals, after consulting the European Parliament. This meant that the ministers of the member states were central to the European legislative apparatus. This would remain the case for several decades to come.

The ministers would meet around the conference table every month, with each member state in turn taking over the role of presidency for a six-month period. The ambassadors would meet once a week in Brussels to prepare the ministerial meetings. This system, known as the Committee of Permanent Representatives, or Coreper, would eventually evolve into one of Europe's most powerful institutions.

The EEC and Euratom treaties have gone down in history as the Treaties of Rome. The treaties take their name from the city where the six countries signed them on 25 March 1957. This photo was taken during the signing session in the Palazzo dei Conservatori on the Capitoline Hill. It shows Konrad Adenauer of West Germany, with, next to him, Walter Hallstein, who would become the first president of the European Commission. Also present are Christian Pineau of France, Antonio Segni of Italy, Paul-Henri Spaak of Belgium, Joseph Luns of the Netherlands and Joseph Bech from Luxembourg. Each one smiled as he took up the fountain pen and put his name to the founding document of European cooperation. Meanwhile, outside the palace, the church bells began to ring.

The treaties were ratified by the six national parliaments without any difficulty. On 1 January 1958, Europe finally came into existence.

Photo:
Signing the Treaty of Rome (left to right): Paul-Henri Spaak and Jean-Charles Snoy et d'Oppuers of Belgium, Christian Pineau and Maurice Faure of France, Konrad Adenauer and Walter Hallstein of Germany, Antonio Segni and Gaetano Martino of Italy, Joseph Bech of Luxembourg, Joseph Luns and Johannes Linthorst Homan of the Netherlands

6

14 January 1962
The common agricultural policy is agreed

Some people will perhaps find this surprising, but the man behind the common agriculture policy was not French. He was a farmer's son from the Netherlands called Sicco Mansholt.

We have to go back to the Treaty of Rome to understand this. The memory of the war – and the hunger it caused – was still fresh in the minds of European governments.[9] They realised the importance of being able to feed their population with their own resources, so they did everything they could to support their farmers. The newly-signed EEC Treaty replaced national agricultural subsidies with a common agricultural policy. Its aim, according to Article 39 was 'to increase agricultural productivity' and 'to ensure a fair standard of living for the agricultural community'. The concrete implementation was left to the Commission, which was asked to come up with the necessary proposals and the ministers of agriculture from the member states, who had to give their consent.

The common agriculture policy (CAP) and the customs union were Europe's first two grand projects. The common agriculture policy was driven forwards by the newly-appointed Commissioner for Agriculture, Sicco Mansholt. In fact, he would have preferred to have been President of the Commission, but this was vetoed by Konrad Adenauer, who declared, 'A farmer and a socialist. That's too much of a good thing.' ('*Ein Bauer und ein Sozialist, das ist des Guten zuviel.*'[10]).[11]

Mansholt drew up an extremely interventionist plan which stated that agricultural prices would be set by political agreements between the member states, and not by market forces. Farmers would therefore be guaranteed European prices for their grain, meat, dairy produce, vegetables, fruit and wine. Moreover, these prices would be much higher than prices on the world market. The difference between the fixed price and the world price would be paid by Europe in the form of import levies (to keep cheap agricultural produce out of the common market) and export subsidies (to ensure that European agricultural overproduction could still be sold on the world market). On 14 January 1962, Mansholt called the six ministers of agriculture to a meeting in Brussels and, after a marathon session, persuaded them to reach an agreement. In

9 The Dutch had been particularly affected by the Hunger Winter of 1944-45, when people were reduced to eating tulip bulbs.

10 Konrad Adenauer, quoted in A. Mozer-Ebbinge and R. Cohen, eds., *Alfred Mozer*, 1980, p. 45.

11 Walter Hallstein of Germany was the first president of the European Commission, which officially launched on 1 January 1958. Sicco Mansholt of the Netherlands, a former farmer and government minister, was appointed vice president and given the agriculture portfolio.

future, the agricultural prices would be fixed annually at the European level.

Mansholt was not an economist. Had he studied economics, he would have known that a system of high guaranteed prices would lead to overproduction. This process was accelerated by technological innovations. Within a short time, Europe was confronted with the notorious butter mountains and wine lakes. These had to be destroyed, in part, to maintain artificially high price levels. Or they had to be dumped on the world market using export subsidies, causing a drop in world prices.

This sparked off protests from agricultural countries that produced more cheaply, such as the United States, Brazil and Australia. Meanwhile, in developing countries, many small local farms were simply driven out of business. As a result, European agricultural policy was sharply criticised. Even in Europe, people could see that European subsidies were going to large agriindustrial concerns and not the small farmer.

The CAP was finally reformed, mainly following pressure from the World Trade Organisation. This resulted in a narrowing of the gap between European prices and world prices for an increasing number of products. In certain cases, the two prices became the same. Instead of price support, the EEC gradually introduced direct support. This gave farmers a sort of basic income that no longer depended on the amount of food they produced. Instead, it increasingly depended on the extent to which they adopted ethical farming methods that took into account the environment, landscape and food quality.

As early as the 1970s, Sicco Mansholt acknowledged the design flaw in his plan. He distanced himself from the policy that he had been instrumental in enacting and became a committed green activist.

Photo:
Sicco Mansholt, founding father of the common agricultural policy

7

14 January 1963
Charles De Gaulle slams the door on the British

Up until the early Sixties, the United Kingdom had no intention of joining the Six. The political and economic ties that bound it with the Commonwealth were much stronger for the British than those that linked them to the Continent. Moreover, the supranational institutions that were enacting European legislation at top speed did not, according to successive prime ministers, fit with the British democratic tradition. And, finally, the British remained sceptical about the long-term survival of the economic community created by the Six.

The upshot was that the British turned their backs on the EEC and negotiated their own European Free Trade Association (EFTA) with the Scandinavian countries, Switzerland, Austria and Portugal. Unlike the EEC's customs union, there was no question here of a common external tariff or anything else with supranational implications. Another important difference was that agriculture played no part in EFTA's structure, whereas a common agricultural policy was an essential element of the EEC for France and the other partners.

In July 1961, an official announcement stated that the British prime minister Harold Macmillan had decided to join the EEC. This unexpected change of heart came as a shock to the Six. But not everyone saw it in a bad light. The Belgian minister Paul-Henri Spaak and his Dutch counterpart Joseph Luns saw British membership as a possible counterweight to the dominant Franco-German axis, which the Benelux countries didn't like. President De Gaulle, however, who had been in power since 1958, was firmly opposed to the idea. Despite leading the French Resistance from London during the Second World War, he remained mistrustful of the 'Anglo-Saxons' and saw them as America's poodles. Moreover, De Gaulle noted, 'You who eat the cheap wheat of Canada, the lamb of New Zealand, the beef and potatoes of Ireland, the butter, fruit and vegetables of Australia, the sugar of Jamaica – would you really consent to feed on continental – especially French – agricultural produce, which would inevitably cost more?'[12]

12 Charles De Gaulle, quoted in Alan Sked and Chris Cook, *Post-War Britain*, 1988, p. 173.

Why then did 'Super Mac' want to burden his country with EEC membership? According to historians, it wasn't the case that Macmillan changed overnight into a federalist. But he saw the British Empire collapsing, and judged that it was in the country's best interests to have a seat at the European table. That would ensure that he knew what was being discussed and Britain could exert its influence to the full in Europe, the United States and the rest of the world. It was no accident that Macmillan had discussed the plan to join the EEC in full with President Kennedy of the United States. Macmillan's plan chimed with Kennedy's dream of a united Europe within a strong NATO. So Kennedy gave Macmillan his full support.

The accession talks were led on the British side by the young deputy foreign secretary Edward Heath. The negotiations began in the spring of 1962, not long after the Six had agreed on the common agricultural policy. The British, of course, were bound by agreements with the Commonwealth, the EFTA countries and their own farmers. The question was, what would they demand in the way of temporary concessions and transition periods.

While the negotiators were doing their best to reach a solution, De Gaulle mounted the podium in the Elysée Palace in Paris. It was 14 January 1963, the start of a new year. De Gaulle spoke without consulting any of the other EEC heads of state or government leaders. His speech emphasised the differences between the Six and the United Kingdom. He also spoke of the danger that Europe, once Britain had joined, would become a 'colossal Atlantic community under American dependence and direction'.

...

Photo:
Charles De Gaulle, during a six-day visit to Germany in September 1962

De Gaulle leaned forward slightly as he spoke these words. 'It is a hypothesis which might appeal to some,' he told his audience, 'but it is not at all what France wanted to do or is doing — which is to create something truly European. Yet it is possible that one day England might transform itself sufficiently to become part of the European community, without restriction, without reservation or preferential arrangement; and in this case the Six would open the door to her and France would raise no obstacle, although obviously England's participation in the Community would radically change its nature and its scope.'

Harold Macmillan was devastated. The five other EEC member states could hardly believe what they were hearing. De Gaulle had slammed the door in Britain's face.

5 February 1963

Van Gend & Loos: a milestone in European legal history

The rules are clear now. European laws are created by the Commission, Council and Parliament. They are directly applicable in national courts without the intervention of parliament. In addition, in the event of a conflict between European legislation and national laws, European law takes precedence.

It all seems logical. Yet it is worth pointing out that this situation is unique in international law. It came about as a result of two important decisions reached by the European Court of Justice in Luxembourg, the body set up by the Treaties of Paris and Rome.

The case was brought before the court in the early Sixties. It involved a Dutch haulage company called Van Gend & Loos which had shipped several tons of urea-formaldehyde from West Germany to the Netherlands. The Dutch customs authorities charged a higher tariff on the imported plastic, whereupon the company appealed to the Dutch national courts. The Treaty of Rome called for the gradual abolition of customs duties and prohibited the introduction of new tariffs. Van Gend & Loos argued that the higher tariff was illegal under European law. The customs authorities countered that the higher tariff was allowed under national laws.

The Dutch judge was perplexed. He turned for advice to the seven judges of the European Court of Justice.[13] Could an individual invoke the Treaty of Rome, a document that only addressed the member states? The general expectation was that the Court would rule in favour of the narrow view. The Six member states had never envisaged such a drastic limitation on their judicial independence. Moreover, the concept of direct applicability was not explicitly mentioned in the European treaties.

But then came the bombshell. On 5 February 1963, the Court of Justice delivered a judgement that legal experts still regard as nothing short of revolutionary. The Dutch president Andreas Matthias Donner stated that: 'the Community constitutes a new legal order of international law for the benefit of which the states have limited their sovereign rights, albeit within limited fields and the subjects of which comprise not only member states but also their nationals.'[14]

13 The Court now has 27 judges, one for each member state.

14 Van Gend & Loos decision, 5 February 1963.

This was indeed revolutionary. It meant that Van Gend & Loos – or any other company, association or individual consumer – could ask for the direct application of European laws. It also meant that national judges became European judges, and were required to apply European laws and treaties in their courtrooms. It may be the case, the Court admitted, that this was not expressly stated in the Treaty of Rome, but it was in the spirit of the agreement.

The German politician Walter Hallstein was president of the European Commission at the time of the decision. He and his colleagues were delighted with the judgement. They had found an ally in the European Court of Justice. The government leaders of the Six were, on the other hand, less enthusiastic, but at the end of the day they accepted the decision of the Court.

One year later, the Court delivered another judgement that has gone down in history. In June 1964, in the case of Costa v Enel, the Court built on the Van Gend & Loos case and ruled that European law took precedence over national law. This principle was subject to some tough examination in the higher courts, but it was eventually accepted by the member states.

This represented a great leap forward in European integration and it was brought about by a seemingly insignificant measure – a judgement pushed through by the European Court.

1 July 1965
The Empty Chair Crisis

On 22 March 1965, the Commission president, Walter Hallstein, put forward an ambitious package of draft legislation. The temporary agreement on the financing of agricultural policy expired on 1 July 1965 and the Six wanted to implement a new agricultural agreement before that date.

Hallstein had just come back from a visit to Washington, where, in his own words, he was treated as 'a kind of Prime Minister of Europe'[15]. He had come up with the idea of combining three different proposals – on the financing of agriculture; on directing all import levies directly to Europe; and, thirdly, on giving European members of parliament in Strasbourg (who were at the time still national representatives) a vote in how that money would be spent. It was an ingenious plan, Hallstein believed. The first proposal would win over member states that had doubts about the second and third proposals. Europe would finally emerge stronger. And his institution, the Commission, would benefit more than any other.

The scene now shifts to the Congress Palace in Brussels, where the Council was meeting on 28 June 1965. Chaired by the French foreign minister Couve de Murville, the meeting had been called to discuss the package put forward by the Commission. The sun was shining outside, but the mood in the meeting room was anything but sunny. Couve de Murville was clearly angry at Hallstein for neglecting to inform the member states about his plans before revealing them to the world. Like President De Gaulle, Couve was not particularly in favour of a federal Europe.

The agriculture proposal was the only one that was desirable, he said. It therefore had to be separated from the others. Giving Europe its own budget was at present entirely out of the question, Couve said. However, three countries – the Netherlands, Italy and Germany (where Chancellor Ludwig Erhard had taken over from Adenauer) – believed it was important for the Community to have its own resources and to give control of them to the parliament.

The brusque way in which De Gaulle had blocked British entry to the EEC was still fresh in their minds. They were in no mood to surrender to further French demands. Belgium and Luxembourg, of course, frantically sought a

15 Hallstein said this following his trip to the United States in March 1965. Quoted in Luuk van Middelaar, *De passage naar Europa*, 2009, p. 88.

compromise. They tried for three days, until time ran out at midnight on 30 June. The month of July 1965 therefore officially began with no agreement having been reached.

At two in the morning, blinded by press flashlights, Couve de Murville announced that the Community was in deep crisis. An exhausted president Hallstein confirmed to the waiting journalists that the meeting had broken up without an agreement. A few hours later, the Elysée Palace announced, ominously, that France had decided on the basis of the situation to take economic, political and legal steps. And then the unthinkable happened. Charles De Gaulle instructed all his country's representatives to leave Brussels. This became known as the Empty Chair Crisis. France's chair was empty and as far as De Gaulle was concerned it would remain empty until the other five countries had admitted their mistake.

Erhard, Luns and Spaak had failed to see this coming. What began as a failed Council meeting had turned into a full-blown crisis that threatened the very survival of the EEC. The question on everyone's lips was: what happens now? There was no precedent in the history of European cooperation for a crisis on this scale. Was De Gaulle really out to sink Hallstein's financial proposal, or was there something more to this crisis?

Coincidence or not, another important deadline was looming. On 1 January 1966, the Six would be taking one further step on the road to unification, as provided for in the Treaty of Rome. From then on, the Council would be able to reach decisions with a qualified majority of votes. It would therefore no longer need unanimity to make binding decisions. The Empty Chair Crisis suddenly took on a different shape.

Photo:
France's empty chair during the European Council meeting in Luxembourg. The French remained absent for seven months following the Brussels Summit.

29 January 1966
The Luxembourg Compromise

In the autumn of 1965, President De Gaulle held a press conference in which he made a series of hostile remarks about the Commission ('some technocratic, stateless and irresponsible group of wise men'), the majority voting rule under the EEC Treaty (a 'mistake of principle') and the risk that this posed for France ('a majority vote would overrule us'[16]). It was clear where he stood. Charles De Gaulle had a problem with the establishing treaty itself. Up until then, decisions were always taken unanimously. De Gaulle wanted to maintain this system, and he was only prepared to return to the European table when the treaty had been amended to take this into account.

De Gaulle confidently assumed that Germany, Belgium and the other three signatory states would activate their bilateral channels, and so one by one (apart perhaps from Joseph Luns of the Netherlands) bow to his demands. But this is not what happened. The five prime ministers from the member states – excluding France – met in Council and decided among themselves that the solution to the problems confronting the Community had to be found 'within the framework of the Treaties and their institutions'[17].

At the same time, the five reached out to France. They proposed the idea of an 'extraordinary' Council meeting without the Commission being present, which might, if necessary, take place somewhere other than Brussels. This could, with the cooperation of the French, find a solution to the crisis.

The French presidential elections were also imminent and the country's largest farmers' union, good for an estimated 20 percent of the electorate, was calling on its members to vote against De Gaulle. The farmers were afraid that the flow of European farm subsidies would be put in jeopardy by the crisis and they didn't like the way De Gaulle was handling the situation.

This proved to be an important lesson for the General. He won the presidential election, but only after a second round that left De Gaulle humiliated. He finally decided to send his minister to the meeting after all. The next part of the story is well known in European circles. On 29 January 1966, the Six met in Luxembourg to sign a compromise, which was in some part due to the conciliatory role adopted by the Belgian Paul-Henri Spaak.

16 Charles De Gaulle, press conference on 9 September 1965, Paris.

17 Council of the EEC, Bulletin CEE 12-1965.

- 'Where,' went the Compromise, 'in the case of decisions which may be taken by majority vote on a proposal of the Commission, very important interests of one or more partners are at stake, the Members of the Council will endeavour, within a reasonable time, to reach solutions which can be adopted by all the Members of the Council while respecting their mutual interests and those of the Community, in accordance with Article 2 of the treaty.
- With regard to the preceding paragraph, the French delegation considers that where very important interests are at stake the discussion must be continued until unanimous agreement is reached.'[18]

This allowed the five member states to announce to their domestic audience, no doubt with some relief, that France would be resuming its seat without in any way compromising the EEC Treaties. The Compromise was simply attached to the Treaties. De Gaulle, meanwhile, was able to announce to the French that he had defended France's right of veto and that French sovereignty remained intact.

18   Luxembourg Compromise, 29 January 1966.

The Luxembourg Compromise, as it was called, would be invoked on other occasions – and not just by France. It has been criticised by many as the stumbling block that has slowed down European decision making for some 20 years. But perhaps it is better to argue that it provided a way out of a crisis that left France absent from the EEC negotiating table for seven months. After all, the ship didn't sink, and France came back on board. It seemed that the six countries were bound together by economic interests that made it difficult for them to break away.

The person who lost most in this crisis was the German Walter Hallstein, president of the Commission. He was not invited to Luxembourg and, in September 1967, when his mandate came up for renewal, was forced to resign following pressure from the French. He was succeeded by the quiet Belgian Jean Rey. The Commission remained weakened for almost two decades, until Jacques Delors took over as president in 1985 and restored its former confidence.

2 December 1969
A new spirit

On 1 and 2 December 1969, the six heads of state and government leaders met in The Hague, the Netherlands, in a gathering that served as a foretaste of the later European Council meetings. Piet de Jong, the Dutch prime minister, served as host and chairman. The venue was the prestigious and magnificent mediaeval Ridderzaal, the Knights' Hall where, for some seven centuries, the nobility of the Low Countries had gathered in all their splendour.

There was, at long last, something to celebrate. What had seemed an impossible dream in the 1950s had finally come to be realised. The Six had abolished customs duties and quotas between the member states. Under the EEC Treaty, the Six were required to implement the changes within a transition period of 12 years, but, due to pressure from the business sector, had managed to achieve this well before the deadline. The Six now dealt with the outside world as a single trading bloc with a common set of tariffs. The member states realised that they carried more weight as a trading bloc than they would have done individually. The Community also had its own agricultural policy, along with competition regulations based on the German model.[19]

A new set of questions now arose. Where should the Six go from here? What form should the next European project take? These issues were on the agenda when the Six sat down in the Ridderzaal on 1 December. The call to action came from President Georges Pompidou of France, who had succeeded De Gaulle in May 1969. He addressed his speech to Willy Brandt, the newly-appointed German Chancellor, along with De Jong of the Netherlands, Eyskens of Belgium, Werner of Luxembourg and Rumor of Italy.

'We are reaching the end of the transition period,' he told the delegates. 'Customs duties are now a thing of the past between our countries. The single market in agriculture has been painstakingly developed. But there are many questions which we need to answer. [...] Are the Six prepared to extend joint action to other fields? Do we or do we not intend to press ahead with the co-ordination of economic and monetary policies, technological co-operation, tax harmonisation, and company law?'

19 The Commission had recently moved into the gleaming new Berlaymont office building in Brussels. The Council also had its headquarters in Brussels, in a new building named the Charlemagne. Both of these institutions had as their address Rue de la Loi (or Wetstraat in Dutch). The name, 'Law Street', was perhaps a subtle hint that more legislation would soon follow.

He continued, 'And I do not forget the very important issue of the membership applications submitted by a number of countries, in particular Great Britain. Now is the time to raise this issue too and to discuss it without preconceived ideas but without giving anything away.[20] [...] In other words, are we prepared to open the door to Great Britain and the other applicants if this means that the Community will be weakened and begin to crumble away? Or do we intend to forge ahead to build a stronger Community, making membership subject to firm undertakings with regard to what has been achieved and what still remains to be done?'

It sounded as if Pompidou was lifting the veto on British membership imposed by De Gaulle in 1963 (and repeated in 1967)[21]. The other five leaders were so excited that they immediately sat down to work on an agreement which was finalised in just two days.

- The agreement provided the Community with its own financial resources. The import duties collected at the external borders would no longer go to the country collecting the duties, but directly to the European institutions. This provided a definitive solution to the financing of the Common Agricultural Policy.
- Economic and monetary union became an official goal.
- The foreign ministers were instructed to come up with recommendations for developing political union. The first step in this direction happened in 1970 with the decision to hold meetings of foreign ministers every six months to discuss global political issues.
- The most tangible result was the resolve to begin accession negotiations with Britain, Ireland, Denmark and Norway. All four countries had been left waiting in line since 1963.

Things were moving at last in Europe. The future looked positive.

20 Georges Pompidou, speech on 2 December 1969, The Hague.

21 Following the veto in January 1963, De Gaulle had blocked a second British request to join the EEC in 1967.

Photo:
The Ridderzaal in The Hague at the start of the EEC Summit on 1 December 1969

1 January 1973
Europe gains three new members

Six months after the summit in The Hague, the official accession negotiations kicked off. Seated on one side of the table was the Community, represented by the six founding members plus the Commission.

There was a good reason for this seating arrangement. During the negotiations preceding De Gaulle's veto, the British had dealt individually with the different member states. The Six wanted this time round to avoid the risk of member states being played off against one another. Hence the show of unity. Facing the Community across the table were representatives from the four candidate member states.

- The United Kingdom. This country was the equal of France and West Germany in terms of economic power and population. The prime minister was Edward Heath, the man who in 1963 had led the UK delegation negotiating EEC membership and who, after De Gaulle's veto, had returned home with the words, 'We in Britain are not going to turn our backs on the mainland of Europe or the countries of the Community.' A successful bid for EEC membership would represent a high point in Heath's political career.[22]
- Ireland. This was predominantly an agricultural country at the time, with an economy that was largely dependent on Britain.
- Denmark. The Danes were only interested in the economic benefits of EEC membership. Their main export market at the time was the United Kingdom.
- Norway. Like Denmark and the UK, Norway belonged to the European Free Trade Association (EFTA). It was keen to follow its main trading partners and join the EEC.[23]

The negotiations were extremely technical and complex – a problem that would only become worse as time went on and the Community grew in size. This is because candidate member states not only have to adapt their tariff structure to conform to Community regulations (eliminating all trade restrictions between member states and implementing the common external tariff); they also have to incorporate all European laws and decisions into their national legislation.

22 Edward Heath finally signed the Treaty of Accession on 22 January 1972 in the Egmont Palace in Brussels. It was not quite the triumph he had hoped. As he arrived for the ceremony, a woman protestor leaped out from the crowd and threw ink over his face. Questioned later by police, the woman turned out to be a German psychologist living in London who was protesting, not at EEC membership, but at a property development in London.

23 EFTA, which was a free trade area, finally had to concede defeat to the more powerful EEC, a customs union. But EFTA still survives with four member states (Norway, Switzerland, Iceland and Liechtenstein).

The negotiations involve the determination of transition periods and occasionally the acceptance of opt-out clauses. In the case of the United Kingdom, for example, the British were given six years to implement the details of the common agricultural policy. The EEC authorities also had to negotiate with the main trading partners of the candidate member states (EFTA in this case) to compensate them for the increased tariffs that would be implemented when the countries joined.

Why did Georges Pompidou, a staunch Gaullist, agree to the accession of the United Kingdom? The change of heart was because of the growing power and confidence of West Germany, where Chancellor Willy Brandt's Ostpolitik was rapidly leading to a normalisation of relations with East Germany.[24] Pompidou was uncomfortable with Brandt's policy and saw the United Kingdom as a useful counterweight to growing German power.

By the end of 1971 the negotiations were drawing to a close. A thick accession treaty was sitting on the table. But first the politicians had to wait for the treaty to be ratified in the national parliaments. The British members of parliament voted in favour of the treaty (with 301 for EEC membership and 284 against). The Irish also supported the legislation (with 83 percent in favour), as did the Danes (63 percent in support). The Norwegians, however, rejected the treaty at the last moment, partly because they were unwilling to share the revenues from their North Sea oil and gas reserves.

On 1 January 1973, three new member states joined the EEC and their staff moved into offices in the Berlaymont and Charlemagne buildings. The Six became Nine. A new chapter in Europe's history had begun.

24 Immediately after he was elected, the social democrat Willy Brandt began negotiations with Moscow, which resulted in a normalisation treaty signed by West Germany and East Germany in December 1971. Brandt was awarded the Nobel Peace Prize in recognition of his efforts.

23 April 1973

Kissinger declares 1973 'The Year of Europe'

The EEC was still coming to terms with its enlargement from six to nine members when, on 23 April 1973, US National Security Advisor (and soon to be Secretary of State) Henry Kissinger, surrounded by burly security guards, stepped onto a podium in New York to deliver a key speech. Following the signing of the Vietnam peace treaty earlier that year in Paris, President Nixon's chief foreign policy advisor had come up with a bold new project. He pulled the speech out of an inside pocket and began to read. It was immediately clear that, now that the United Kingdom had joined the EEC, the White House was looking more closely at Europe. The speech was called 'The Year of Europe'. It defined 1973 as the year in which the Atlantic alliance would be revitalised and the values and goals linking Europe and the United States would be clarified.

'Nineteen seventy-three is the year of Europe because the era that was shaped by decisions of a generation ago is ending,' Kissinger told his audience. 'The revival of western Europe is an established fact, as is the historic success of its movement toward economic unification. [...] In the forties and fifties the task was economic reconstruction and security against the danger of attack; the West responded with courage and imagination. Today the need is to make the Atlantic relationship as dynamic a force in building a new structure of peace, less geared to crisis and more conscious of opportunities, drawing its inspirations from its goals rather than its fears.'[25]

25 Henry Kissinger, 'Year of Europe,' speech on 23 April 1973, New York.

Kissinger proposed 'revitalising' the Atlantic relationship and working more closely in economic relations (trade) as well as defence. He noted that the US maintained troop levels in Europe, but that 'Europe is not carrying its fair share of the burden of the common defence'. He also suggested that Europe and the US could work together in areas such as ensuring the supply of energy and building long-term relations with oil-producing countries. 'This could be an area of competition, it should be an area of collaboration,' he concluded.

This gave the Nine something to think about. How should Europe reply to Kissinger's question? And who, in fact, was able to speak to Nixon's government on behalf of Europe? It certainly wasn't the Commission, whose civil servants were only employed to deal with trade and other technical portfolios. The Council of Ministers, likewise, could only deal in areas linked to the common market.

Kissinger made it clear that he wanted to deal with political leaders, not technocrats. 'They must engage the top political leaders, for they require above all a commitment of political will,' he told his New York audience.

Did that mean that the 'top political leaders' could negotiate on behalf of Europe? This question received a nuanced answer from German Chancellor Willy Brandt during a dinner at the White House. 'None of us meets you any longer solely as the representative of his own country but at the same time already, to a certain degree, as a representative of the European Community as well. So, I, too, am here not as the spokesman *of* Europe, but definitely as a spokesman *for* Europe.'[26]

In his memoires, Kissinger formulated the key weakness of Europe's position. 'If every European leader was a spokesman for Europe but could not represent it, and those who represented Europe were civil servants with no authority to negotiate, who then could act authoritatively?'[27]

Kissinger's Year of Europe turned out to be a flop. This wasn't just because the Watergate scandal broke later that year, leading to Nixon's downfall. Europe didn't have someone at the top whom Kissinger could call. It couldn't give a clear answer. This became painfully obvious when the oil crisis broke out at the end of 1973.[28] There was no sign of a common European response as each state selfishly focused on ensuring that its own energy reserves were protected.

26 Willy Brandt, quoted in Henry Kissinger, *Years of Upheaval*, p. 157.

27 Henry Kissinger, *Years of Upheaval*, p. 157.

28 The OPEC boycott only affected the Netherlands, along with the United States.

Photo:
Portrait of Henry Kissinger taken on 21 September 1973, one day before he was sworn in as Secretary of State

Kissinger's question was posed again by a journalist in 2009 at a press conference announcing the appointment of the Belgian Herman Van Rompuy as the first permanent president of the European Council. 'Kissinger asked what number he should call to speak to Europe,' the journalist said. 'Who should president Obama call to speak to Europe?'

The silence was broken by Van Rompuy, who replied in English: 'I am anxiously waiting for the first call.' The press room erupted into laughter. But then Barroso intervened: 'Now there is no doubt – the secretary of state of the United States should call Cathy Ashton because she is our foreign minister'.

So now everyone knew. Even 37 years on, the question Kissinger put to Europe was far from being resolved. It still wasn't clear who could speak on behalf of Europe. In fact, as we will argue later, it had become more complicated.

14

10 December 1974
The European Council is created

The European Council saw the light of day in the 1970s. This was a period that Jean Monnet described as 'the years of patience'. The new institution brought together the heads of state or government of the different member states for regular meetings.

The European Council came into existence on the initiative of Giscard d'Estaing, who became French president following the death of Georges Pompidou. Germany also had a new leader, Helmut Schmidt, following the resignation of Willy Brandt.[29] Giscard and Helmut were able to communicate with one another without the need for an interpreter and quickly became the best of friends. The Franco-German juggernaut was back on the road again.

In September 1974, President Giscard d'Estaing invited his fellow leaders to talk over issues at an informal lunch in the Elysée Palace. 'Informal' was the magic word. Giscard d'Estaing was well aware that they would be suspicious of his proposed new body. The Benelux countries, for example, believed that the existing EEC structure (an independent Commission, Council of Ministers and a European Parliament) was the best structure to protect their national interests within Europe. The smaller EEC countries were far from keen on meetings where the large countries could impose their will. But who could refuse a glass or two of fine French wine? Moreover, everyone realised that Europe was getting bogged down and it was time for something to be done.[30]

The 'picnic summit', as it was known, took place, but the leaders didn't get much further than concluding that they could take on more European responsibilities themselves. Giscard d'Estaing, backed by Schmidt, argued in favour of a regular meeting of heads of state and government to break the deadlock on difficult issues. The Dutch leader Joop den Uyl and the Belgian Leo Tindemans were among those who opposed the move. They preferred to put the emphasis on measures to strengthen the Commission. But the Franco-German juggernaut was unstoppable. On 9 and 10 December 1974, the EEC leaders were invited once again to the Elysée Palace, this time to discuss the situation in the Community and the decisions that had to be taken. The setting was carefully orchestrated by Giscard d'Estaing – comfortable armchairs, a blazing log fire. This formed an elegant backdrop to the new agreement:

29 Willy Brandt stepped down in May 1974 after one of his close advisers, Günter Guillaume, was exposed as an East German spy.

30 The challenges were enormous: high oil prices, stagnating economies and monetary instability. In his inaugural speech, US president Gerald Ford didn't even mention Europe.

- The heads of state and government would in future meet three times a year to resolve 'internal problems' in the European decision-making process, as well as discussing 'external problems' in which Europe had a stake;
- The national leader in the role of rotating president at any given time would represent the member states in matters involving the outside world;
- One meeting every year would be held in Brussels or Luxembourg. This measure was proposed by Belgian prime minister Leo Tindemans, who wanted to see it tied in more closely with the European institutions;[31]
- The president of the European Commission would attend all meetings (a demand of the Benelux states) and a report of each meeting would be presented to the European Parliament.[32]

Notice that the term 'European Council' appears nowhere in the formal conclusions; the term was still a sensitive issue for the smaller member states.[33] But this didn't stop Valéry Giscard d'Estaing from using it. When he emerged from the meeting, the press pack pounced on him, hungry for a soundbite. He gave them just what they wanted: 'Le Sommet est mort,' he announced triumphantly. 'Vive le Conseil Européen!' – 'The summit is dead. Long live the European Council.'

31 In 2000, the Belgian prime minister Guy Verhofstadt successfully lobbied for all ordinary meetings of the European Council to be held in Brussels.

32 Closing Communication at the Paris Summit.

33 Legally speaking, the European Council was not a genuine European institution. It only became so 35 years later, with the signing of the Lisbon Treaty.

Photo:
Photograph taken at the Elysée in Paris on 10 December 1974: (left to right) Leo Tindemands of Belgium, Helmut Schmidt of Germany, Gaston Thorn of Luxembourg, Harold Wilson of Great Britain, Aldo Moro of Italy, Valéry Giscard d'Estaing of France, Cearbhall Ó Dálaigh of Ireland and Joop Marten den Uyl of the Netherlands

15

7 June 1979

The European Parliament is elected by the voters

34 MEPs now divide their time between two parliament buildings in Brussels and Strasbourg, spending three weeks every month in Brussels and one week in Strasbourg, where the plenary sessions are held.

35 The British might have been expected to veto this decision, but Labour prime minister Harold Wilson had just announced a referendum on whether or not to remain in the EEC, which meant his hands were effectively tied.

36 This is one of the greatest paradoxes in the history of the European institutions: while the European Parliament has gained more power over the years, voters' enthusiasm has fallen off sharply.

The European Parliament met for the first time in 1952, although at that time it was called a 'Common Assembly' rather than a parliament. It was created following pressure from West Germany and met in the French city of Strasbourg on the Franco-German border.[34] Defined under the first European treaty, it was originally an indirectly-elected assembly of MPs drawn from the national parliaments. Although it is one of the oldest common institutions, it had little impact in the early years of the EEC. The parliamentarians were originally restricted to offering non-binding advice on draft European legislation. Later on, they had the power to propose budgetary amendments, which were then enacted by the Council of Ministers.

The term 'Assembly' showed that there was reluctance, at least in some quarters, to entertain the idea of directly-elected parliamentarians who might one day lord it over the member states. The French in particular were for a long time hostile to the idea of direct elections. De Gaulle and Pompidou both refused to use the term 'parliament' when they talked about the Strasbourg Assembly. The British, too, were reluctant to use the name. Mrs Thatcher, who came to power in May 1979, absolutely refused to utter the P-word and resolutely referred to the body as 'the Assembly'.

But what about the provision in the Treaty of Rome (article 138) calling explicitly for 'elections by direct universal suffrage'? Up until the early 1970s, every attempt to implement this measure was met with a firm French *non*. A window of opportunity opened in late 1974, when, as we saw in the previous chapter, president Giscard d'Estaing was desperate to create a European Council. So he persuaded the Benelux countries to support the bid by promising them direct European elections in return.[35] Four years later, the new voting system was approved.

On 7 June 1979, the citizens from the nine EEC member states went to the polling stations for the first time to elect European members of parliament. They turned out in large numbers to cast their votes. The turnout in 1979 reached 63 percent, which was 20 percent higher than the depressingly low figure of 43 percent registered in the most recent elections, in June 2009.[36]

The new parliament was composed of 410 members and, for the first time in its history, appointed a woman as president – Simone Veil, a French woman who had been imprisoned as a child in Auschwitz concentration camp. Its members would, from now on, be elected every five years and belong to large pan-European political groups (Christian Democrats, Socialists, Liberals, environmentalists) or various smaller groups. The specialised parliamentary committees, which now form an important part of the parliament's work, were already present in 1979. Their role, then as now, is to scrutinise draft legislation proposed by the Commission. In the early days, however, the role of parliament was limited to giving advice, which the Council was free to accept or reject. The introduction of direct elections marked the first step in the creation of a fully-functioning parliament. Over the course of several decades, the European Parliament has gradually taken on new powers, so that it can now shape legislation, and function, at least in some ways, as a proper law-making body with an increasingly powerful role in Europe.

The French socialist and economist Jacques Delors, then 54 years old, was one of the MEPs elected in June 1979. The press reports from the time describe Delors as taking to his new working environment like a duck to water. He was appointed chairman of the committee on economic and monetary affairs – one of the most powerful committees in the parliament. This gave him an influential role in the supervision of the European Monetary System (EMS) – the fixed-but-adaptable exchange rate system set up by Giscard d'Estaing en Helmut Schmidt in January 1979 to stabilise currency fluctuations. In his report, Delors declared himself in favour of the EMS, as well as the theoretical European currency then called the ecu – the forerunner of the euro.

Photo:
Simone Veil (in the centre) is elected president of the European Parliament

16

29 November 1979
Mrs Thatcher demands her money back

On 4 May 1979, the United Kingdom's first female prime minister walked through the door of her new official residence at 10 Downing Street, head held high, famous handbag firmly clasped. Margaret Thatcher came to power with an overwhelming majority. After five years of Labour government, the British people were expecting great things from the new prime minister.

Elsewhere in Europe, many government leaders were pleased by Thatcher's victory. 'A refreshing change,' noted France's Valéry Giscard d'Estaing. 'I am particularly impressed by her knowledge, authority and sense of responsibility,' Germany's Helmut Schmidt declared.[37]

Neither could have been aware of the bomb she was about to drop on the European project. It happened in Dublin, where the nine EEC heads of state and government leaders met on 29 November 1979. A second oil crisis had flared up, and Europe had not yet been able to find a solution.

'I want my money back.' Her handbag landed with a loud thud on the conference table. 'I must be absolutely clear about this,' she continued. 'Britain cannot accept the present situation on the budget. It is demonstrably unjust. It is politically indefensible: I cannot play Sister Bountiful to the Community while my own electorate are being asked to forego improvements in the fields of health, education, welfare and the rest.'[38]

The core problem was the 1 billion pounds sterling that, according to Thatcher's calculation, the United Kingdom was expected to pay to Europe in 1980. Bear in mind that the European Community had been given its 'own resources' in the 1970s. Since then, the EEC coffers were filled every year with customs duties collected at external borders, with agriculture levies and a small part of VAT revenue.[39] The money was spent mostly on propping up the common agriculture policy.

Like Germany, the United Kingdom contributed more each year to the EEC budget than it received in return. 'It is unthinkable that I should accept such a situation,' said Thatcher. 'I want back what I put in, I demand a fair repayment.'

37 Helmut Schmidt, quoted in Alan Sked and Chris Cook, *Post-War Britain*, 1988, p. 376.

38 Margaret Thatcher, quoted in Alan Sked and Chris Cook, *Post-War Britain*, 1988, p. 376.

39 Since 1988, the member states have contributed to the budget according to their Gross Domestic Product (GDP). In 1988, it also became customary to draw up a budget for several years, rather than just one.

The EEC budget was no longer relevant to the present day, she argued. It made no sense for Europe to play the role of agricultural cartel. The wine lakes and butter mountains produced by EEC subsidies were an absurdity. It would get even worse, she continued, if countries like Greece, Spain and Portugal, which were then negotiating to join the EEC, eventually became members. There would soon be olive oil seas and lemon mountains.

Schmidt tried gently to explain that the EEC's entire budget comprised no more than one percent of the total gross national product of all the member states. In the light of this, he argued, Thatcher's deficit was a small price to pay. In return, the UK gained access to a gigantic export market which benefited the country's industries. Giscard d'Estaing argued that the notion of a fair return was not a concept that had any meaning in a community. He called on her to take a broader view and work on ideas that would serve the common interest.

The arguments didn't convince her. Thatcher was proud to call herself the Iron Lady – a name she was given by the Russians. She didn't budge one inch from her position, and the Dublin Summit ended in a complete fiasco. The European leaders flew back to their capitals without any agreement. The EEC had lost some of its shine.

Photo:
Margaret Thatcher holding her famous handbag

45

17

26 June 1984
The Fontainebleau Agreement

The nagging question of the British rebate hung over Europe like a dark cloud for the best part of four and a half years. The United Kingdom had been receiving an annual 'cut' in its payments since 1980, but this wasn't enough to keep Thatcher quiet. She wanted a fundamental change to the system, and made that perfectly clear to the new European leaders – Mitterrand of France, Kohl of West Germany, Craxi of Italy, Lubbers of the Netherlands and Martens of Belgium. In 1984, Thatcher decided that the budget debate had been dragging on long enough. She demanded a permanent solution. If no solution was reached, she said, I will let the EEC go bankrupt. This was no idle threat. In 1984, the Community no longer had the financial means to support its growing agriculture subsidies. If the EEC wanted to increase its own resources, it would need a unanimous vote. That meant Thatcher had to agree.

The photograph shown here was taken on 26 June 1984 in front of the imposing Château de Fontainebleau, where the French kings once stayed while they were hunting in the Fontainebleau woods. The photograph shows, from left to right, Adréas Papandréou of Greece (which had joined the EEC as its tenth member on 1 January 1981), Poul Schlüter of Denmark, Pierre Werner of Luxembourg, Garret Fitzgerald of Ireland, Margaret Thatcher (smiling slightly at the successful outcome of her strategy), François Mitterrand of France (as holder of the rotating presidency, he was placed neatly in the centre), Bettino Craxi of Italy, Ruud Lubbers of the Netherlands, Wilfried Martens of Belgium, Helmut Kohl of West Germany and, finally, Gaston Thorn of Luxembourg (president of the Commission). There was a palpable sense of relief in the air on that sunny day in the French countryside. The host, Mitterrand, had shown inspiring leadership and an agreement was signed that commentators would describe as 'historic'.

After years of squabbling, the Ten had sat down in Fontainebleau castle and agreed on a broad range of issues.

- The United Kingdom would get back a large part of its contribution: £600 million in 1984, and thereafter 66 percent of the difference between the UK's contribution in VAT receipts and its share in expenditure;

- Agricultural expenditure would be limited through quotas and levies;
- All member states would contribute a larger percentage of VAT to the European budget (1.4 percent instead of 1 percent);
- The accession negotiations with the new democracies of Spain and Portugal (which had stalled because of the question of agricultural subsidies) could now go ahead, leading to the accession of Spain and Portugal some 18 months later, on 1 January 1986.
- A new committee was established (the Dooge committee, modelled on the Spaak committee set up to prepare the ground for customs union) whose aim was to formulate proposals for closer European cooperation in all areas. This led in March 2005 to proposals on the introduction of majority voting and political union.

During the meeting at Fontainebleau, a discussion took place between Mitterrand's minister of finance, Jacques Delors, and the new German Chancellor Helmut Kohl. It didn't form part of the official conclusions, but it was nevertheless an important and revealing exchange.

'Welcome, Mr Kohl,' said Delors.

'Thank you,' said Kohl. 'I'm glad to meet you here. Now, with regard to the next president of the Commission, I would agree to a French president, as long as his initials were JD and not CC.'[40]

This marked the beginning of a close friendship between Jacques Delors and Helmut Kohl that would last many years. It was an immensely important relationship that would shape the future integration of Europe.

40 Charles Grant, Brussels correspondent for the Economist, chronicles this meeting in his book *The House that Jacques Built* (1994). Kohl was deeply impressed with Delors, who played a key role in the successful outcome of the Fontainebleau summit. The initials CC stood for Claude Cheysson, the French foreign minister.

Photo:
Heads of state and government posing in front of the Château de Fontainebleau

18

7 January 1985

Jacques Delors takes over the Commission

41 In Delors' day
    the Commission
    employed 17,000
    civil servants. The
    figure has now
    risen to some
    25,000, which
    is still relatively
    modest compared
    to the number of
    staff employed by
    national and local
    administrations
    across Europe.

42 To take an example,
    the Belgian Com-
    missioner Willy De
    Clercq was res-
    ponsible in 1985
    for trade. His
    role was to give
    political guidance
    to the Directorate-
    General for Trade.
    Within each DG, the
    Director-General is
    the top-ranking civil
    servant. The rela-
    tionship between
    Commissioner and
    Director-General is
    one that can lead to
    conflict, as well as
    gossip, each time a
    new Commission is
    appointed.

On 6 January 1985, Jacques Delors entered the Berlaymont building on Brussels' Rond-Point Schuman/Schumanplein as the European Commission's eighth president. His office was located, as were the offices of all his cabinet members, on the thirteenth floor, the highest in the neighbourhood (on the gounds that the president should always be able to see what his civil servants are getting up to).[41] Delors was a highly strategic thinker as well as being a self-made man. He brought with him from Paris a portrait of Jean Monnet, who had died in 1979. Delors had the deepest respect for Monnet and hung his portrait in pride of place on his office wall. He also brought his friend Pascal Lamy, whom he appointed as his chef de cabinet. Lamy was given more or less a free rein in the running of the Commission. He shook up the soporific bureaucrats with such energy and drive that he immediately earned himself the nickname Exocet, after the French guided missile that had been used by the Argentinian army a few years earlier to sink a British cruiser during the Falklands war.

The Commission currently has 27 members, one for each member state. When Delors took over as president, there were 17 Commissioners, since larger member states were at the time entitled to two. This photograph shows the Commissioners sitting around the meeting table on the thirteenth floor, alongside the secretary-general who sets the agenda and takes the minutes. Each of the Commissioners seated at the table was responsible for one particular policy area and had his or her own Directorate-General, or DG, staffed by European civil servants.[42] The president – referred to by most civil servants as 'Monsieur le Président' – was responsible for ensuring that the European ship was sailing in the right direction, as well as serving as the public face of the Commission in its dealings with the outside world.

The key role of the Commission was (and still is) to come up with proposals for laws that would apply across Europe. The process begins with a DG preparing a particular proposal, which, in a process known as Inter Service Consultation, is then submitted to all DGs for their comments. The proposal then goes to the Commissioner's cabinet where the political impact is assessed.[43] It is at this point that national interests come into play, although, strictly speaking, the Commission is supposed to be independent and work towards a common European good. When the Commissioners sit down for their weekly meeting every Wednesday morning, their *chefs de cabinet* will normally have already fought over and won the necessary compromises. The proposal simply has to be formally accepted, so it can begin its passage through Parliament and Council.[44]

But what legislative proposals should the Commission now put forward? This is a question to which Delors devoted a great deal of attention. The European idealism of the founding fathers had almost vanished by the early 1980s, leading to what was called, in the jargon of the time, 'Eurosclerosis'. This reflected the widely-held belief that Europe was a lethargic museum culture that could hardly hope to compete with the dynamism of the United States or Japan. Business leaders complained that the common market promised to them by the Treaty of Rome was still nothing more than a fiction. While, admittedly, governments had abolished customs duties and quotas, they had found less obvious ways of protecting their national markets (for example, by imposing technical standards).

Delors went on a tour of all the national capitals with the aim of finding out what project would help to put Europe back on track. Institutional reforms? The common market? More political cooperation, perhaps? A monetary union? The only project that won the vote of each of the member states was the common market. So Delors now knew what he had to do. He went straight to the office of Francis Arthur Cockfield, usually known as Lord Cockfield, the British Commissioner for the Internal Market, and delivered his message. 'My dear Lord Cockfield, we have a job to do'.

43 This takes place in the weekly meetings, or *hebdos*, of the chefs de cabinet, held on Mondays. The chef de cabinet of the president (at that time Pascal Lamy) plays a crucial role. He or she can, behind the scenes, wield more power than a good many of the Commissioners.

44 This is termed an *A Point*, where all that is required is a rubber stamp to turn the text into an official Commission proposal. Proposals where debate is needed are referred to as *B Points*, but these are rare.

Photo:
Willy De Clercq of Belgium during the appointment of the new Commission

19

14 January 1985
Delors launches Project 1992

On 14 January 1985, Jacques Delors told the European Parliament that he planned to get rid of every internal border in Europe by the end of 1992. This was the first time he referred to the date '1992', which over the years would acquire mythical proportions. There is still a degree of uncertainty about who came up with the intelligent notion of linking this brand-new project to a fixed date, doing for the single market what the Treaty of Rome had done for the customs union. Lord Cockfield, author of the famous White Paper on the completion of the internal market, claimed that he had chosen the deadline. ('You don't say, let's start building a factory. You decide when you want it running by.') [45] According to Lamy, the slogan '1992' first saw the light of day during a cabinet meeting when Delors' maiden speech was being drafted. Whatever the truth, there was an eight-year gap between the beginning of 1985 and the end of 1992 – precisely the length of two Commissions. [46] That was the reason for the deadline, according to both Cockfield and Lamy.

The plan begged many questions. What did it mean exactly to remove internal borders? What regulations were needed to create a genuine single market – could the Commission perhaps be a little more precise? The Commission did at least take note of that final point: it made clear that its role was to be the political motor of European integration and to develop concrete policies. In June 1985, the 68-year-old Lord Cockfield presented his White Paper, which caused a political storm in Europe. The plan was far more ambitious than any of the commentators had expected and contained at least 280 proposed laws that had to be implemented if a genuine single market – comprising free movement of goods, services, people and capital – was to be realised. This free market idealism went much too far for even the arch-liberal Margaret Thatcher, who had confidently sent Cockfield to Brussels in the belief that he would support her vision of the single market. 'Cockfield has gone native', she complained loudly. [47] Relations between Thatcher and Cockfield never really recovered.

Cockfield's proposed route to the internal market was set out in three lengthy chapters, covering everything from the elimination of the irritating frontier controls within Europe (removing the need for customs documents

45 Arthur Cockfield, cited in *Europe relaunched*, Nicholas Colchester and David Buchan, 1990, p.29.

46 The Commission now remains in office for five years, but in Delors' day it was one year less.

47 Margaret Thatcher, cited in *Europe relaunched*, Nicholas Colchester and David Buchan, 1990, p.31.

and physical checks on people, plants and animals) to the removal of fiscal obstacles to free trade (simplification of VAT payments within Europe).

The chapter on the 'Elimination of Technical Barriers to Trade' included the new and radical principle of 'mutual recognition'. This principle stated that a product that conforms to the legal requirements in one country can legally be sold anywhere in the internal market, as long as it conforms to the minimum safety requirements (which would be determined by the European Communities).[48]

If it had its way, the Commission would also apply the same rules to services (banking, insurance companies, etc) and to employees, so that a single passport or diploma would be sufficient to work across the entire European Communities. Likewise, public contracts would be open to any company based anywhere in Europe. This was a big step forward for the member states and called for considerable trust in each other. 'They want an open internal market', said Cockfield firmly when he set out his plans. 'Well, they have got it.'[49]

It is ironic that this profoundly liberal plan was pushed through by Jacques Delors, a committed socialist. He ordered his departments to calculate how much the various hidden barriers to trade cost Europe every year. They came up with the figure of 200 billion Ecu[50] and then worked flat out to convince businesses and governments of the enormous advantages of the project.

As far as Delors was concerned, '1992' wasn't just a measure to improve Europe's performance in the global economy. The internal market would also, he reasoned, push Europe to a new level of integration. He was right in that respect: when the heads of state and government met in Milan in July 1985 to discuss these plans, there was already a new sense of purpose in the air.

48 This principle was based on a 1979 ruling by the European Court of Justice known as the Cassis de Dijon decision, in which the Court held that Germany could not prohibit the import of a French fruit-flavoured liqueur on the grounds that it contained a different alcohol percentage.

49 Arthur Cockfield, cited in Europe re-launched, Nicholas Colchester and David Buchan, 1990, p.29.

50 According to the calculations of a team of economists led by Paolo Cecchini.

Photo: Jacques Delors speaking for the first time as Commission president at the European Parliament in Strasbourg

20 | *29 June 1985*
Craxi pulls off a coup

On 28 and 29 June 1985, the ten European leaders met in the impressive Castello Sforzesco in Milan. The weather was warm and sunny. The prime ministers of Spain and Portugal had also been invited to attend, as their countries were about to join the EEC. Jacques Delors was also present, representing the Commission. The meeting was hosted by the socialist prime minister Bettino Craxi, president of the Council, assisted by the Italian foreign minister Giulio Andreotti (nicknamed 'the fox'). Two main points were on the agenda:

- Approval for Project 1992;
- A discussion of the unanimity rule of voting and whether in the light of the single market it would be better to abolish it. The Dooge Report was quite clear on this point: Europe would have to introduce qualified majority voting if it was to be revitalised, especially with the accession of Spain and Portugal. It seemed as if the time might be right to call an intergovernmental conference to discuss changes to the Treaty of Rome.

Delors expected to get the go-ahead for his White Paper. This had already been made clear in the countless meetings he had held with the member states. But he didn't expect to make any headway in the plan to introduce qualified majority voting. Delors was up against three prime ministers who were set against any tampering with the Treaty of Rome: Poul Schlüter of Denmark, whose national parliament would not allow him to surrender any power to the Community; Andreas Papandréou of Greece, who wanted to use his veto to secure European cash; and – who else? – Margaret Thatcher, who as usual was refusing to budge an inch. She was prepared to give her minister more leeway in the discussions if that helped bring about free competition, but embarking on discussions that might lead to a change in the treaty was a bridge too far. She wouldn't even discuss the matter. A gentlemen's agreement would have to do.

But things turned out rather differently, thanks to the cunning of Craxi. This caused enormous relief among those who wanted a change in the treaty (Martens, Lubbers, Santer, Craxi himself, Fitzgerald, Kohl and, after some soul-searching, Mitterrand). Everyone was poised to pack their bags and head off home without an agreement when Craxi asked his colleagues to vote. He reminded them of the content of article 236, which stated that an intergovernmental conference could be called by a simple procedural decision based on a majority of votes in favour.

Calling for a formal vote, unannounced, on the basis of a forgotten article in the treaty – this was something that had never happened before in the ten-year history of the European Council. Up until then, the aim had always been to work towards unanimity. But on 29 June 1985, the vote was forced through in the face of opposition. The result came as no surprise: seven in favour and three against. Craxi ordered fireworks to be set off above the castle to symbolise the victory he had pulled off – there would be an intergovernmental conference to introduce changes to the Treaty of Rome.

What Craxi achieved that Saturday was a risky strategy. 'A coup d'état!', complained Papandréou. Schlüter of Denmark referred to it as 'rape'[51], while Thatcher stormed off in a fury. She gathered up her papers and left in such a foul temper that her fellow prime ministers seriously wondered if she would ever return to the European conference table.

Craxi had gambled on the fact that the British had so much to gain from the single European market that Thatcher would eventually be forced to change her mind. The gamble paid off. When the intergovernmental conference began two months later in Luxembourg, all the member states were present at the table. When the Single European Act was finally signed, no one used their veto to oppose it. Thatcher, Schlüter, Papandréou – they all put their name to it. Proving, once again, that you should never underestimate an Italian when it comes to the art of negotiation.

51   Quoted in Luuk van Middelaar, *De Passage naar Europa*, 2009, p. 153.

Photo:
Portrait of Margaret Thatcher taken in the 1980s

21

17 February 1986

The Single European Act changes the Treaty of Rome

The intergovernmental conference set up to amend the Treaty of Rome began with a series of meetings in September 1985. This meant that the foreign ministers of the member states [52] and their diplomats met repeatedly in Luxembourg throughout that country's presidency in the second half of 1985.

The Commission has no official role in an 'intergovernmental' conference, but Jacques Delors nevertheless played a hugely influential role in the enactment of the Single European Act. According to his own account, he and his team were responsible for drafting 85 percent of the text that was finally ratified. Other sources put Delors' contribution at some 70 percent.[53] No other European treaty amendment was so deeply influenced by the Commission.

Delors fired off one text after another to the member states. Here is the first of his many contributions: 'The Community shall adopt measures with the aim of progressively establishing the internal market over a period expiring on 31 December 1992.'[54] This measure particularly pleased the British, who were keen for the deadline of 1992 to be stated in writing. Delors also proposed other chapters in the treaty covering environment, research and development, measures to combat economic and social inequality (such as funding for the poorer countries), and the European Parliament.

The European Parliament? Delors realised that the fact that the Council could now make decisions on the basis of qualified majority voting meant that the national parliaments would lose a certain degree of decision-making power. He proposed granting the European Parliament some influence on the Council through a cooperation procedure. Kohl found this a fantastic idea.

Delors also worked on a chapter dealing with a possible monetary union, which he saw as a logical extension of the single market. He waited before introducing it until the main elements of the new treaty were finally in place in November. In his biography, Charles Grant quotes Delors as saying: 'It's like the story of Tom Thumb lost in the forest, who left white stones so he could be found. I put in white stones so we would find monetary union again.'

It seems odd that the Single European Act, which the member states signed on 17 February 1986, was greeted with extreme indifference by the public and dismissed by the Economist as 'a smiling mouse'. In fact, it was a small masterpiece which had some far-reaching consequences.

52 They included Germany's Hans-Dietrich Genscher, France's Roland Dumas and Italy's Giulio Andreotti, along with Britain's Europe minister Linda Chalker.

53 Charles Grant, *Delors*, 1994, p. 75.

54 Single European Act, article 8A.

- From now on, the Council would take decisions on the single market by qualified majority vote.[55] The veto culture introduced by the Luxembourg Compromise, along with the all-night meetings that often achieved nothing, was now a thing of the past in the case of the internal market.[56] This meant that the Commission could draft proposed legislation with renewed enthusiasm, since there was now a strong chance that the proposal would be adopted;
- The cooperation procedure ensured that the European Parliament had a voice which the Council had to take seriously. While this wasn't a fully-fledged right of codecision, it was nonetheless a huge step forwards;
- The Community was given new policy areas for the first time since its creation in 1957, extending its influence to environment, research and development. In addition, one chapter was devoted to the possibility of achieving monetary union at some point in the future;
- The member states pledged to 'endeavour jointly to formulate and implement a European foreign policy', and to 'inform and consult each other on any foreign policy matters of general interest'.[57] This 'European Political Cooperation in the sphere of foreign policy' was equipped with a secretariat based in the Council building in Brussels, even though it was strictly speaking separate from the European Community.

The Single European Act, which entered into force in July 1987, gave a much-needed boost to the process of European integration. 'I knew that if this treaty was accepted, it was an important moment and that historians would one day recognise the value of this mouse,'[58] said Delors at a later date.

55 Qualified majority means that countries are allocated votes in accordance with the size of their population.

56 The unanimous vote rule continued to apply in the case of decisions involving tax, workers' rights and free movement of people.

57 Single European Act, article 30.

58 Jacques Delors, quoted in Charles Grant, *Delors*, 1994, p. 75.

Photo:
The Single European Act, with the signatures of Leo Tindemans of Belgium, Uffe Ellemann-Jensen of Denmark, Hans-Dietrich Genscher of Germany and Karolos Papoulias of Greece

22

A blueprint for economic and monetary union

59 Valéry Giscard
d'Estaing, quoted in
Nicholas Colchester
and David Buchan,
Europe relaunched,
1990, p.164.
There were only
eleven currencies
at the time because
Belgium and
Luxembourg shared
the franc.

60 A revealing study
carried out before
the introduction of
the euro revealed
that a tourist who
set off with 1,000
Belgian francs in his
wallet and changed
currency in each
of the 12 member
states would return
home with just half
of the initial sum.

In 1988, with the deadline for Project 1992 fast approaching, the European member states revisited the issue of the single European currency, which had been rather neglected. Giscard d'Estaing, former president and co-founder of the European Monetary System, complained loudly: 'Who ever heard of a single market with eleven currencies?'[59] He was quite right. With the single market about to become a reality, both companies and citizens were asking whether it would not be easier to have a single European currency. Companies would find it easier to plan investment decisions, and they would save conversion costs. Tourists would no longer have to go to the bank to stock up with pesetas or lira, nor would they end up being ripped off by bureaux de change.[60]

There were other factors in play which motivated countries such as France and Italy to work towards a single currency. But Germany, with its stable Deutsche Mark and low inflation rate, was noticeably less enthusiastic, while Thatcher, needless to say, was utterly opposed to the plan. Under the EMS, the German Bundesbank in Frankfurt had evolved into a central bank that dictated monetary policy to everyone else. For some time now, this had annoyed certain countries, especially the French. Moreover, the free movement of capital in Europe – one of the cornerstones of Project 1992 – was now being implemented. The European member states (including the United Kingdom) had agreed to abolish controls on the movement of capital on 1 July 1990. If capital could be moved unimpeded across national frontiers, it was clearly going to be difficult for any country to implement a national monetary policy.

In June 1988, the government leaders decided to investigate whether they would ever be in a position to implement an economic and monetary union – based on a single European currency, a single monetary policy determined by a European Central Bank, and the requisite economic coordination. A proposal was formulated to bring all the governors of the central banks around the table to draw up a sort of blueprint. Chancellor Helmut Kohl agreed with the idea and suggested that the proposed committee should be chaired by none other than Jacques Delors, who was just beginning his second term of office as president of the European Commission. This was a highly unusual choice, since the president of the Commission normally had nothing to do with monetary policy. It shows, once again, how much trust Kohl placed in a certain person whose Christian name began with J and whose surname began with D.

Thatcher was not enthusiastic, but she did not put her foot down, since she believed that nothing concrete would follow. The central bank governors, notably Karl Otto Pöhl of the German Bundesbank, were firmly set against such a project.

On 17 April 1989, Jacques Delors proudly presented the bank governors' report to the ministers of finance. It contained the following recommendations:

- Phase 1: to begin on 1 July 1990, when controls on movement of capital are abolished. All the currencies are placed in the EMS. The central banks begin to work together more closely and the member states move towards economic convergence;
- Phase 2: date to be decided. Transition period. A European Central Bank prepares the ground for monetary union and issues guidelines as regards the implementation of monetary policy. The exchange rates are kept within stricter margins. The ministers of finance monitor each other's economies more closely;
- Phase 3: date to be decided. The exchange rates are irrevocably fixed. The common currency replaces the national currencies. The European Central Bank – an independent body with various roles, the main one being to maintain price stability – determines monetary policy. Binding budgetary rules are introduced to control government deficits.
- What this calls for: a change in the treaty.

Delors, who was passionate about monetary affairs, had persuaded all the bank governors (including a reluctant Pöhl) to move in the direction he proposed. The Delors Report and the launch of Phase 1 were approved by the member states during the Madrid Summit, in June 1989. This blueprint for economic and monetary union contained many elements that eventually found their way into the Treaty of Maastricht in 1992.

Yet Mrs Thatcher remained fiercely opposed. 'This would be the biggest transfer of sovereignty we've ever had,' [61] she warned.

61 Margaret Thatcher, quoted in Nicholas Colchester and David Buchan, *Europe relaunched*, 1990, p. 173.

23 | *7 October 1989*
Gorbachev's kiss

A series of events in 1989 ultimately led to a cataclysmic upheaval in Europe and the rest of the world. The Germans called it *die Wende*, the change. It came about following a thaw in Soviet relations with the West (*glasnost*) and economic turmoil within the Communist Bloc. The result was nothing less than the collapse of the Communist system.

The process began in Poland in January 1989, when the Solidarity trade union, led by Lech Walesa, gained official recognition. For the first time ever, legitimate opposition was allowed in Eastern Europe.

The revolution spread to Hungary, where many were still haunted by the memory of Soviet tanks rolling into the country in 1956. Free elections were introduced in March, leading to the departure of the ruling Communist élite.

In May, the dissident Czech writer Vaclav Havel was released from prison. In the June elections held in Poland, Solidarity won a landslide victory, seizing all but one of the seats in the Sejm, or lower house of the Polish parliament. On 27 June, the new Hungarian minister of foreign affairs Gyula Horn joined his Austrian counterpart Alois Mock on their common border to cut the barbed wire that had separated their countries during the Cold War. By now the whole world was waking up to the fact that the division of Europe was rapidly coming to an end.

The changes kept coming at a dizzying pace. In July 1989, Austria, which had been neutral, announced that it wanted to join the European Communities. In August, a 'singing revolution' erupted in the Baltic states with a human chain of singers linking Estonia, Latvia and Lithuania. A short time later, some 10,000 East Germans managed to escape via Hungary and the West German embassy in Prague. In September, the Slovenians voted to change their constitution to allow them to break away, which marked the beginning of the end for Yugoslavia.

On 7 October, the German Democratic Republic celebrated its 40th anniversary. On that day, a photographer took this historic photograph during the celebrations in East Berlin. As Gorbachev headed down Unter den Linden, Berlin's main thoroughfare, the crowds lining the street started shouting out 'Gorbi, help us!' At that moment, he turned to Erich Honecker, the Communist party leader and head of state, and gave him a kiss. It was a kiss that carried a clear message. Gorbachev knew that the GDR's days were numbered and he had no intention of intervening to prop it up. 'Life punishes those who come too late,' he told Honecker, who was forced to step down a mere 11 days later.[62]

How did the EEC leaders respond to these momentous events that were taking place in the countries to the east? Helmut Kohl was over the moon, but his enthusiasm wasn't shared by the other 11 leaders. His colleagues were nervous and confused. They were afraid that this would endanger the delicate postwar balance between East and West. And, of course, they were afraid that Germany would once again become a dangerous power.

Jacques Delors was also taking these events seriously. Ten days after Gorbachev's kiss, he gave a speech in the College of Europe in Bruges that many regard as one of the best he ever made.

'History is accelerating. Communist Europe is exploding under our very eyes. Gorbachev launches perestroika and glasnost. Poland and Hungary undertake political reforms aimed at more freedom and democracy. East Germany (the GDR) is shaken by the flight of tens of thousands of its citizens who take refuge in the Federal Republic of Germany. The contagion of freedom has now reached Leipzig and East Berlin. [...] As many European leaders have already stressed, it is the European Community, a Community of laws, a democratic structure, a dynamic economy, which acted as an example and a catalyst for these developments. It is not the West which is drifting towards the East, but rather the East that is attracted by the West.'[63]

62 Mikhail Gorbachev, quoted in Geert Mak, *In Europe*, 2008, p. 716. Hoenecker stepped down on 18 October 1989.

63 Konrad Adenauer had talked about the concept of 'magnet Europa' as early as the 1950s.

Photo:
Mikhail Gorbachev kissing Erich Honecker in East Berlin

Will the European Community be up to tomorrow's tasks? This is the question we must ask ourselves, whether we are talking about supporting the economic modernisation of the Eastern countries, which is an essential condition for the success of their political reforms, or about the need to address, in due time, the German question. [...] History is accelerating. We must accelerate as well. [...] I have always been a practitioner of the policy of small steps [...] I stray from it somewhat today, because our time is limited. A quantum leap is required, both in terms of the structure of the Community and in our modes of external action. [...] I hope that we will be able to repeat, within the coming two years, the words spoken by another great European, Paul-Henri Spaak, when the Treaty of Rome was signed: 'This time, Western men did not lack boldness and did not act too late'.'

Delors gave this speech in the College of Europe, where just one year earlier Margaret Thatcher had stood on the podium to deliver her famous 'Bruges Speech'. During the address, she had noted: 'It is ironic that just when those countries such as the Soviet Union, which have tried to run everything from the centre, are learning that success depends on dispersing power and decisions away from the centre, there are some in the Community who seem to want to move in the opposite direction.'

She then rejected the idea of a European superstate. 'We have not successfully rolled back the frontiers of the state in Britain, only to see them re-imposed at a European level with a European superstate exercising a new dominance from Brussels.'

9 November 1989
The Berlin Wall comes down

24

'Mr Gorbachev, open this gate! Mr Gorbachev, tear down this wall!' President Ronald Reagan said during a speech in West Berlin in 1987. He was standing in front of the Brandenburg Gate, which had been cut off from West Berlin since the wall went up. Reagan's advisers pressed him to cut out this sentence. They were afraid of offending the Soviet leader. But Reagan kept it in his speech, in the hope that he could push Gorbachev into acting. Reagan was no longer president when the wall finally came down on 9 November 1989, but we can assume that he relished the moment.[64]

This is how it happened. On Thursday 9 November, the GDR leaders decided to relax travel restrictions to West Germany. The pressure at the frontier posts had simply become too great to contain. One of the most powerful party leaders, Günter Schabowski, held a press conference that evening that was broadcast live. Without having properly read the brief, Schabowski announced that East Germans could now travel to West Germany without any problem.

'Does that also apply to West Berlin?' a West German journalist asked. 'And when does this come into effect?' All the heads in the room turned to look at Schabowski. He started shuffling through the papers in front of him in search of an answer. 'Ab sofort,' he replied with a shrug. 'Immediately.' The room fell silent. Then all the journalists rose to their feet and rushed to their computers and telephones. Schabowski's reply could only mean one thing, they decided. The Berlin Wall, which had divided the city since 1961, was coming down.

One of the first East Germans to taste freedom described the feeling in his diary as he drove through the checkpoint.

'Dream and reality were mixed up. The border guards let us through. The girls cried. They huddled together on the back seat of the car, as if they were afraid of an air raid. We drove across the death strip that had divided the city for 28 years and suddenly we saw West Berliners. They were waving, cheering and shouting. I drove along Osloer Strasse to my old school, where I gained my certificate in 1960. Suddenly, Astrid asked me to stop the car at the next crossroads. She just wanted to stand on the street. Touch the ground. Like Armstrong after landing on the moon. She had never been to the West.'[65]

That night, Berlin was one big party. People rushed to the checkpoints, some-

64 By that time, Reagan had been replaced by Georges Bush senior.

65 Werner Krätschell, quoted in Geert Mak, *In Europe*, 2008, p. 717.

times still in their pyjamas. In Moscow, Gorbachev was being strongly advised to send Soviet troops to Berlin. He knew it was pointless. The tide had turned.

The fall of the Berlin Wall marked a turning point for the European Community. Up until that moment, each of the member states had its own point of view on the collapse of the Communist Bloc. But 9 November was a wake-up call for the 12 members of the EEC. There were now some urgent questions that needed a collective response. One question was whether it was possible to convert a command economy, with no concept of private property, to the Western model. Another question was whether the two Germanies could be peacefully reunited. And, following on from that, whether it was in fact desirable to have a large and powerful Germany at the heart of Europe.

66 Jacques Delors speaking on German television, 12 November 1989.

A West German TV station gained an interview with Commission president Jacques Delors, who had grown up in the 1930s with the idea that Germany was the great enemy of France. 'What do you think about the idea of Germany becoming one country again and East Germany as a result becoming de facto a member of the European Communities?' He replied in German: 'Ich habe keine Angst' – 'I am not afraid'. He went on to tell the German audience: 'You have done so much for Europe. Stay with us. Together we can realise a beautiful vision.'[66] This sealed the friendship between Kohl and Delors forever. Kohl would never forget that Delors, unlike Thatcher or Mitterrand, embraced the idea of German unity from the day the wall came down.

Photo:
Crowds surge through the Berlin Wall at Potsdamerplatz on 10 November 1989

9 December 1989
Monetary union in return for German reunification

On 8 and 9 December 1989, Europe's heads of state and government gathered for a summit in the French city of Strasbourg. The mood of the meeting, chaired by François Mitterrand, was extremely bitter. The old bond of friendship that had always existed between France and Germany had suddenly vanished. In the words of Chancellor Helmut Kohl: 'This was the most hostile summit of my entire career.'[67]

What was the matter? On 28 November – just before the European summit – a triumphant-looking Kohl had stood up in the packed Bundestag and set out the future of Germany as he saw it. He wanted to achieve reunification as soon as possible, and had drawn up a ten-point plan to bring this about.

Kohl was well aware that this was a highly sensitive issue. Yet he had neglected to warn his European colleagues about his plans before the summit. He had told Bush, who had given his approval. But that was all. This did not go down well with the leaders of the former occupying powers – France and the United Kingdom – or indeed with any of the other EEC leaders.

Moreover, Kohl had neglected to refer in his speech to the Oder-Neisse border laid down in 1945 to separate East Germany from Poland. This had given Poland a large area of former East Prussia. In an interview with the Dutch author Geert Mak, Lubbers recalled his meeting with Kohl:

'What would you have done? Were we supposed to wholeheartedly support German reunification? And what then? Would the new Germany renounce its claims on former East Prussia? Historians are completely wrong if they say that in 1989 no one contested the Oder-Neisse frontier with Poland. There were still strong political elements within Germany that would have been only too happy to see the old situation restored. There were still major conflicts simmering away between Germany and the rest of Europe.'[68]

Given the political situation, it's hardly surprising that Kohl kept his ten-point plan secret from the other EEC leaders. Both Thatcher and Mitterrand had made trips to the Soviet Union after the fall of the Berlin Wall to share their concern with Gorbachev. They were hoping that he would put a stop to any thoughts of German reunification.

67 Helmut Kohl, quoted in Syp Wynia, 'Mislukte samenzwering', in *Elsevier*, 7 November 2009.

68 Ruud Lubbers, quoted in Geert Mak, *In Europe*, 2004, p. 986.

69 Wilfried Martens,
    De Memoires, 2006,
    p. 617.

70 Conclusions of
    the Strasbourg
    European Council
    Summit, 8 and 9
    December 1989.

71 So Mitterrand
    achieved in mon-
    etary union (making
    the German Mark
    into a European cur-
    rency) what Schu-
    man had achieved
    in 1951 for coal and
    steel. See Luuk van
    Middelaar, *De pas-
    sage naar Europa*,
    2009, p. 260.

72 Margaret Thatcher,
    quoted in in Syp
    Wynia, 'Mislukte
    samenzwering', in
    Elsevier, 7 Novem-
    ber 2009.

With all this bickering, the Strasbourg Summit unsurprisingly turned out to be a tense affair. 'Thatcher spoke out against unification,' wrote Belgian prime minister Wilfried Martens in his memoires.

'Mitterrand hesitated. So did Andreotti. Gonzalez, Santer and I were in favour. Lubbers chipped in: 'Looking back at the past, is it such a good idea to make Germany one nation again?' Kohl was furious at Lubbers' insinuation. 'I will teach you German history!' he snarled at Lubbers after dinner. [69] No wonder Ruud Lubbers failed to land Europe's top job in 1994 when he was put forward as a candidate to succeed Delors as president of the Commission.

The fact that, despite all this, the Strasbourg Summit turned out to be a success, is due to the firm leadership of Mitterrand. Kohl gave his formal agreement for a European currency, thereby guaranteeing that Germany would remain more firmly committed to Europe than ever (over the past months Kohl had tried to postpone discussions on monetary union). In exchange, Mitterrand provided the political declaration that Kohl was looking for:

'We seek the strengthening of the state of peace in Europe in which the German people will regain its unity through free self-determination. This process should take place peacefully and democratically, in full respect of the relevant agreements and treaties and of all the principles defined by the Helsinki Final Act, in a context of dialogue and East-West cooperation.'[70]

This historic agreement was reached exactly one month after the fall of the Berlin Wall. It gave France monetary union, while it allowed Germany to become a reunited sovereign state.[71] But not everyone was happy with the deal. At the end of the summit, Thatcher made a bitter observation. 'We beat the Germans twice, and now they're back.'[72]

Photo:
Group photo taken after
the Strasbourg Summit

3 October 1990
Germany is reunited

Thatcher, Mitterrand and Lubbers totally misjudged the speed of German re-unification, which was achieved in a remarkably short space of time. As early as 10 February 1990, Helmut Kohl had flown to Moscow to talk to Gorbachev. At that time, Gorbachev was preoccupied with the break-away of the Baltic states, and he allowed Kohl to go ahead with his plan to create a single state (gratefully accepting the billions of Deutschmarks offered in financial aid).

On 14 February, a decision was taken to hold talks on the external aspects of German reunification. This involved the four post-war occupying powers (United States, United Kingdom, France and the Soviet Union) together with the two German states – 'Four plus Two,' as it was called. The Germans immediately changed it to 'Two plus Four'.

The first free elections in East Germany ended with a resounding victory for Kohl's CDU party.[73] The people voted in huge numbers for federal democracy, freedom of the press, the rule of law and, of course, the Deutschmark. In April, Kohl recognised the Oder-Neisse frontier with Poland and, on 1 July, the Deutschmark was introduced into East Germany. Two weeks later, a crucial announcement came out of Moscow: Gorbachev had agreed to let reunited Germany become a member of Nato. On 31 August, West Germany and East Germany signed the Unification Treaty and, on 12 September, the final '2+4' treaty was ready to be signed in Moscow. It all happened in less than one year.

Did this mean that Kohl was no longer thinking about the question of Europe? Not at all. Kohl was once described by the influential Europe analyst Timothy Garton Ash as 'the most formidable politician – and statesman'[74] of his time. Here he proved it. He wanted to do more than simply tie his country to Europe in an economic and monetary sense. Kohl was convinced (even more so than his great role model Adenauer) that Germany should not stand alone in the heart of the European continent. Its history and sheer size made that undesirable.

'Not a German Europe but a European Germany,' was Kohl's motto. Kohl was in favour of granting more power to the European Parliament. He also pushed for a Europe with a stronger political role. This formed the basis for

73 On 18 March in neighbouring Czechoslovakia, the former dissident writer Vaclav Havel had already been elected president.

74 Timothy Garton Ash, *History of the present*, 1999, p. 148.

75 Quoted in Luuk van
    Middelaar, *De pas-
    sage naar Europa*,
    2009, p. 265.

76 Kohl didn't invite
    any of his European
    colleagues to the
    festivities, although
    Jacques Delors was
    among the guests,
    as was Enrique
    Baron, at the time
    president of the Eu-
    ropean Parliament.

77 Geoffrey Howe, res-
    ignation speech in
    the House of Com-
    mons, 13 November
    1990.

a Franco-German proposal that was sent out to the other EEC leaders: 'Given the enormous changes taking place in Europe, the completion of the internal market and the achievement of economic and monetary union, we believe that it is necessary to speed up the political construction of the Europe of Twelve. [...] We think that the time has come for us to transform the relations between the member states into a European Union.'[75]

An intergovernmental conference on economic and monetary union was already planned, but Kohl and Mitterrand wanted to add a parallel conference on political union. This proposal was greeted enthusiastically by the European institutions and the leaders of the Benelux countries. They had long been arguing that it was time for a fundamental change in the way that Europe worked. The plan was rapidly pushed through at the Dublin Summit. Thatcher continued to say, 'No, no, no,' but she was increasingly isolated within Europe.

This was roughly the situation in Europe on 3 October 1990, when the German Democratic Republic ceased to exist and 16 million former East Germans – including the young physicist Angela Merkel – became citizens of a new united Germany.[76] They immediately became members of the European Community, which shifted its frontier on the same day from the Elbe to the Oder.

Two months later, Kohl won the first German post-reunification election. By then, Thatcher had made her exit from the political stage. She resigned on 22 November 1990, after her own party had declared that her anti-Europe rhetoric was 'running increasingly serious risks for the future of our nation'[77]

Thatcher was succeeded by the grey figure of John Major. European summits would be somewhat less dramatic without the Iron Lady.

Photo:
Waving to the crowds
from the Reichstag in
celebration of German
unification: (left to right)
Hans-Dietrich Genscher,
Hannelore Kohl, Helmut
Kohl and Richard von
Weizsäcker

30 September 1991
The Dutch back the wrong horse

In 1991, the European member states launched the two government conferences that would eventually lead to the Maastricht Treaty. At the first, the member states' finance ministries were expected to prepare the treaty amendments required for economic and monetary union; while at the second their foreign ministries would give shape to the political dimension that they wanted for the Union. As regards the common currency, the situation was clear: it was going to happen, largely along the lines dictated by Delors and the governors of the central banks. The political dimension was more nebulous and complex. There were several special requests that had been put forward: a common foreign and security policy (requested by France, Germany, Belgium and Spain); greater powers for the European Parliament (Germany, Italy and the Benelux countries); more social policies (the preceding countries plus France); European citizenship (proposed by Spain); more co-operation in the policy areas of home affairs and justice (this was requested by Germany, which had been flooded with asylum seekers following the fall of the Berlin Wall). It was up to the country holding the presidency of the European Council (Luxembourg up until the summer, followed by the Netherlands until the end of the year) to find a way through this minefield.

In April 1991, Luxembourg proposed a draft treaty in which all these different elements were incorporated. The document put forward three different types of rules or 'pillars': the first pillar involved Community affairs, including economic and monetary union; the second involved foreign and security policy; and the third was devoted to justice and home affairs. The pillars were developed by the French representative Pierre de Boissieu, who married into the family of Charles De Gaulle and still wields considerable power in the Brussels administration.[78] The Commission, Parliament and Court of Justice would play a far smaller role in the second and third pillars than in the first. If you were to place a pediment on top of the pillars and carve the words 'European Union' on it, then you would have something resembling a Greek temple. The British described it as 'a beautiful design' – as did the French, Danes and Portuguese. The Belgians and the Dutch, along with Delors, were less enthusiastic: they didn't want a temple but rather a tree, with a single trunk

78 De Boissieu now serves as secretary-general of the Council of Ministers.

(the Commission and Parliament doing more on every front) and branches spreading out in all directions.[79] In June 1991, at about the same time as the first shots were being fired in former Yugoslavia, the Twelve decided to adopt Luxembourg's three-pillar proposal as the basis for the new treaty.

And then the Netherlands took over the presidency. Minister Hans van den Broek, who had his hands full dealing with the crisis in Yugoslavia, delegated a large part of the treaty negotiations to Piet Dankert, state secretary for European affairs in the Dutch government. He was a former president of the European Parliament, as well as being a close friend of Jacques Delors.

79   Delors had put forward a concrete proposal along these lines, but this was rejected by the Luxembourg presidency. The analogy of temple versus tree was made by the Belgian prime minister Mark Eyskens.

80   Peter van Walsum, quoted in Luuk van Middelaar, *De passage naar Europa*, 2009, p. 268.

81   Luuk van Middelaar, *De passage naar Europa*, 2009, p. 269.

Dankert took a deep draw on his cigarette, threw the Luxembourg text in the rubbish bin, and wrote a new draft treaty that excluded the three pillars and confined both home and foreign policy within the straitjacket of the Community. 'It's a better proposal,' announced Van den Broek when he presented Dankert's text to his European colleagues on 30 September 1991. Given the fierce debate on this question that had raged for several months among the Twelve, the Dutch initiative seemed to reflect, according to one Dutch diplomat, 'an astonishing level of wishful thinking'.[80]

'Out of the question', was the response from all the other member states, with the exception of Belgium (Mark Eyskens was the only one to support Van den Broek). The Dutch were left out in the cold. The tree was chopped down *sofort*, *immédiatement* and *subito*. The three pillars were restored as the fundamental architecture of the Treaty of Maastricht.

The Dutch learned two important lessons on that day:

- A president should take note of the consensus and not push their own position;
- The member states are not prepared simply to hand over control of their foreign and security policy. There is still an overwhelming consensus that responsibility for these issues cannot be assumed by civil servants in Brussels or members of the European Parliament in Strasbourg. It is one thing to create a common market, the Dutch writer and philosopher Luuk van Middelaar argues, but quite another matter to make decisions on the deployment of troops or police officers.[81] Van Middelaar is right. He understands the way that Europe works, which is presumably why Herman Van Rompuy, president of the European Council, appointed him in 2009 as his policy adviser and speech writer.

10 December 1991
The European Union is born in Maastricht

On 9 and 10 December 1991, Dutch minister-president Ruud Lubbers welcomed his European colleagues in Maastricht's Provinciehuis. This striking building, home to the Limburg provincial government, is located on an island in the River Maas. It was here that the leaders of the Twelve gathered to approve the Maastricht Treaty, or, to give its official title, the Treaty on European Union. For Lubbers, this was the perfect ending for the Dutch presidency.

The signing on 10 December 1991 marked a big step forward for the Twelve. What had begun in 1957 as a plain customs union was now referred to in grand terms as a 'European Union'.[82] This was, admittedly, based on three distinct 'pillars', but it still represented a huge step forwards. So what were the main points in the treaty that was approved on that island in the Maas?

- *A single European currency*. Economic and monetary union (EMU) was seen as the crowning achievement of the internal market. Monetary Union would be introduced in three phases with completion on 1 January 1999 at the latest. Countries could only belong to EMU if they satisfied four criteria: low inflation, a low interest rate, a low national debt (not greater than 60 percent of the gross domestic product, or GDP) and a low ratio of government deficit to GDP (not greater than 3 percent). The famous 'Maastricht criteria' were incorporated into the treaty to satisfy German demands. Countries with a large government deficit were thus forced to make deep spending cuts. The United Kingdom and Denmark insisted on the right to keep their currencies out of the EMU.
- *The Community would take on new policy areas and reach more decisions on the basis of majority voting*. Now that the single market was almost completed, the Community could extend the scope of its policies. It gained responsibility for policy areas such as trans-European networks (transport, telecommunications, energy), industrial policy, consumer protection, education, youth and culture. Social policy, which was a non-starter for the British (at least under prime minister John Major), was dealt with in a separate protocol.[83] Majority voting was extended to new policy areas (such as environmental legislation), even though it was still doubtful

82 The Treaty of Maastricht did not confer legal personality on the European Union ; this only happened in 2009 under the Treaty of Lisbon.

83 Britain's Tony Blair finally signed up to the social chapter in 1997.

84 The Treaty of Maastricht therefore included a revision clause: a new intergovernmental conference was held in 1996.

85 The co-decision procedure works as follows: if the members of the European Parliament vote to reject a proposal by the Council, then a mediation committee is set up comprising members of the Parliament and the Council. If there is still no agreement, then the proposed legislation is scrapped. But if an agreement is reached, then both Council and Parliament have to approve the text.

whether this would be sufficient in the event of new states joining the EU (which, everyone now agreed, was going to happen very soon). [84]

· *The European Parliament was granted the right of codecision.* A new codecision procedure was introduced in several policy areas (internal market, consumer protection, etc) which allowed Parliament to make decisions on the same footing as the Council.[85] This was greeted with enthusiasm by members of the European Parliament. At the same time, MEPs were given a role in the appointment of the European Commissioners for the first time.

· *The introduction of the idea of European citizenship.* This defined the rights and duties of nationals of the member states, including the right of free movement across the entire EU, the right of residence, the right to vote in local and European elections in the country of residence, diplomatic and consular protection provided by other member states when a citizen is outside the EU in a country where their own country has no representation, the right to petition the European Parliament and the right to submit complaints to a European ombudsman. All of these measures were introduced by the Spanish prime minister, Felipe Gonzales, a fervent supporter of European integration.

· *The development of a common foreign and security policy (known as the second pillar)*, with member states agreeing 'to safeguard the common values, fundamental interests and independence of the Union.' This assigned

Photo:
Queen Beatrix of the Netherlands posing with President Mitterand of France (front row, left) and the other European leaders at Neercanne castle, near Maastricht. The leaders include Ruud Lubbers (front row, right) and Helmut Kohl talking to Jacques Delors (second row, middle).

responsibility for supervising the common foreign and security policy to the European Council and included the provision that it could eventually lead to a common defence policy. This was the first time that terms like these had been uttered since the failure of the European Defence Community back in 1954.

- *The development of a common policy on home affairs and justice (the third pillar)*. Member states agreed to co-operate in areas such as asylum, immigration and anti-terrorism, although each decision required a unanimous vote (as was the case with the second pillar).[86]

The Maastricht Treaty may have been a great leap forward, but there was one serious problem – it was virtually unreadable. Perhaps this was why the treaty, which the Twelve happily signed in Maastricht on 7 February 1992, only scraped through the ratification process by the skin of its teeth.[87] It finally came into force on 1 November 1993.

86 Voting by qualified majority only applied in the case of visa policy.

87 It scraped by in France with just 51% voting in favour. The Danish initially rejected the treaty, but it was passed in a second referendum.

29

22 June 1993
The door is open

Once upon a time, there was a country called Yugoslavia. You could see it from Italy. It wasn't democratic and it wasn't particularly rich, but it still had a fairly good reputation. Children born in Yugoslavia might come from different ethnic backgrounds, but they grew up thinking of themselves as simply Yugoslav.

But then the Iron Curtain disappeared, and something went terribly wrong in Yugoslavia. When Slovenia declared independence in June 1991, fighting broke out for the first time. This initial struggle lasted ten days. Croatia then followed suit and declared independence. Germany recognised the new state just before the Maastricht Summit, without any prior discussion.[88] A war broke out in the region that lasted until well into 1992. The most violent phase of the conflict erupted in April 1992, when the city of Sarajevo (where the First World War broke out in 1914) was besieged by Bosnian Serbs. This led to enormous suffering in the civilian population, including rape, ethnic cleansing and mass executions. While all this went on, the European Union simply stood on the sidelines and watched.[89]

It is hardly surprising, therefore, that the atmosphere was tense when Europe's leaders met on 22 June 1993 in Copenhagen. 'For a year and a half I've been absolutely sapped by this Yugoslav business,' said Delors, who had travelled to the Danish capital for the event, despite suffering from serious back pain at the time. 'I have a bad conscience that I cannot do anything about these events, which stresses me.'[90] The atrocities in the Balkans and Europe's inability to produce a collective response weren't the only questions that preoccupied the Twelve. They also had to decide what to do about all those Central European countries that had been eagerly knocking on the door of Europe since the fall of the Berlin Wall.

Most of the member states agreed – and Delors concurred – that it was still too early to talk about membership. After forty years of Communist central planning, the simple fact of the matter was that these countries, which had only just begun to create capitalist market economies, were not yet ready. There was also the question of whether the Treaty of Maastricht made the European Union strong enough and sufficiently cohesive to allow it to absorb

88 Hardly a promising start for Europe's common foreign policy.

89 The collapse of Yugoslavia led to 150,000 dead and two million people driven from their homes.

90 Jacques Delors, quoted in Charles Grant, *Delors*, 1994, p. 291.

so many new countries. The United Kingdom and Germany were the only countries that had argued since the fall of the Berlin Wall in favour of rapid accession, although they had different reasons for doing so. The other member states were against. The United Kingdom saw expansion as a way to turn the Union, in the words of Delors, into 'a market without a soul'. Germany had already absorbed the former GDR and had everything to gain from having stable and prosperous neighbours to the east.

The argument that expansion would protect each country's own national security finally won the day. During the Copenhagen Summit, the Twelve declared that they were in principle in favour of the accession of the new member states. At the same time, they laid down the criteria which the candidate member states had to fulfil to quality for membership. These became known as the Copenhagen criteria:

- Political criteria: the country must have a stable legal system and strong institutions; it must be democratically organised; it must respect human rights and protect minorities;
- Economic criteria: the country must have an efficient market economy;
- Legal criteria: the candidate member states must incorporate the complete body of Community law – known as the *acquis communautaire* – into their national legislation.[91] This was no small matter, as European legislation at the time ran to some 90,000 pages.

91 Candidate countries are also expected to commit themselves to adopting the European currency.

What the Twelve were effectively saying was this: if you become like us, you can come and join us at our table. Within the relatively short time span of 14 years, a total of 15 new (and not so new) countries managed to achieve this. They made enormous changes to conform to the entry requirements of the European Union. You can't deny that this was a highly successful example of EU foreign policy.

DANMARK 1993

Photo:
The Copenhagen Summit

30

15 December 1993
The Uruguay Round ends in success

World trade is a complex and sometimes surprising policy area. Trade, whether in goods or services, is one area where the Commission has a lot of room for manoeuvre. It is always the Trade Commissioner who has to deal with the outside world in the name of the European Union,[92] following guidelines set down by the member states. At the end of the day, the member states – and the European Parliament – have to give their approval. 'I have never been in an environment that combines bare-knuckle political arguments and technocratic detail in quite the same way,' confessed former Trade Commissioner Peter Mandelson in his blog.

Who does a Trade Commissioner sit with at the conference table? Sometimes it is with countries that were formerly colonies of the member states. These countries were traditionally granted preferential access to the European market and are now gradually opening up their own markets. Sometimes it is with countries bordering the Mediterranean, where Europe is trying to create a meaningful free trade zone. Or it is with candidate member states that have been signing one free trade agreement after another in preparation for EU membership. In addition to all this, the Commissioner negotiates bilateral free trade agreements with countries beyond Europe where the EU wants to remain competitive, such as Mexico and Mercosur, or, more recently, South Korea, India, Singapore, Malaysia and Canada.

For any Commissioner wanting to flaunt his negotiating skills, there is no better place to do so than in the multilateral discussions on opening up world trade. The negotiations normally take many years,[93] and they almost never go smoothly. The Uruguay Round began in Punta del Este at the end of 1986 as a sort of Project 1922 for the whole world. But, after seven years of talks, it became bogged down because of an unresolved conflict between the United States and Europe. The problem, as is often the case, could be traced back to the agriculture sector. The Europeans could not promise the Americans and the rest of the world that they would dismantle the system of agricultural subsidies. (The French threatened to invoke the Luxembourg Compromise during the negotiations.) This led to huge arguments: Delors (who originally followed the French line) clashed with his Commissioners (who saw that an agreement

92   During Delors' period as Commission president, the post was occupied by, respectively, the Belgian Willy De Clercq, the Dutch Frans Andriessen and the British Sir Leon Brittan. Since the beginning of 2010, the Belgian Karel De Gucht has occupied the position.

93   The Kennedy Round lasted from 1962 to 1967, the Tokyo Round from 1973 to 1979, and the Uruguay Round from 1986 until the end of 1993. The Doha Round began in 2001 and there is still no end in sight.

was almost within reach); the French ('non') clashed with the British, the Germans and the Dutch ('come on!'); the Europeans ('our farmers are dead set against any deal') fell out with the rest of the world ('it's a scandal!').

It all finally worked out thanks to the sheer willpower of the European and American negotiators (in particular Leon Brittan and Mickey Kantor), as well as pressure from the business sector, which had been lobbying hard for a successful outcome. Jacques Delors also played a role by selling the final deal to the French. He defended the agreement by asking: 'What is the aim of GATT on agriculture? It's that the two elephants who monopolise the market, the United States and the Community, leave some space for the developing countries.'[94] In making this statement on French TV, Delors effectively put an end to his political career.

94   Jacques Delors, quoted in Charles Grant, *Delors*, 1994, p. 177.

The agreement was finally signed in Geneva on 15 December 1993. It reduced industrial import duties by an average of 40 percent, scrapped textile quotas, opened up agricultural trade and created for the first time a multilateral framework for the service sector and intellectual property rights. It also established the World Trade Organisation (WTO), based in Geneva, which could issue binding judgements in cases involving disputes between trade partners. The agreement helped considerably to stimulate the global economy, create new jobs and provide the consumer with greater choice as well as lower prices. The current Doha Development Agenda is taking place against the background of a new world order in which China, India and Brazil play an increasingly important role. The talks have stalled, but we have to hope that they will finally reach a successful conclusion, helped along by EU Trade Commissioner Karel De Gucht and WTO Director-General Pascal Lamy, Delors' former chief of staff and former EU Trade Commissioner.

Photo:
Pascal Lamy

31

25 June 1994
Who will succeed Jacques Delors?

In 1994, Jacques Delors was nearing the end of his third term as Commission president. He was tired. 'I became the symbol of an idea of Europe which is in the process of vanishing. I am discouraged to the extent that I can no longer be useful. I can no longer stamp my mark on Europe, it's finished.'[95]

Who was going to be picked as the new Commission president? Observers were placing their bets on Ruud Lubbers, the man with the bushy eyebrows, who had started his third term as Dutch prime minister in 1989. Lubbers initially denied that he was in the running for the job. But he had his supporters. During the Edinburgh summit in 1992, he had shown great flexibility when Spain had come to the EU asking for more money, so it was no surprise when the Spanish prime minister Felipe Gonzales announced in May 1994 that Lubbers was a candidate. This was later confirmed by The Hague.

Delors had already sounded him out, said Lubbers, and he was happy to see him take over the baton. But it was up to the other prime ministers to make the final decision. This was due to happen at the end of June 1994 during the Corfu Summit. But then Helmut Kohl threw a spanner in the works. The German Chancellor had never forgiven Lubbers for backing Thatcher on the issue of German reunification at the 1989 Strasbourg Summit. He definitely didn't want Lubbers as president. After the Berlin Wall fell, Lubbers had dared to suggest that, in the light of recent history, it was possibly not a good idea for Germany to become one country once again. Kohl believed that Lubbers had no right to speak out on this issue. To make matters worse for Lubbers, he had argued that the European Central Bank should be located in Amsterdam rather than Frankfurt (a ploy that failed) and that a Dutch person should be given the top job. He did get his own way with the job appointment: the Dutchman Wim Duisenberg became the first president, rather than Hans Tietmeyer of Germany. This had piqued Kohl, who thought he had already conceded enough when he gave up the Deutschmark.

The two men clearly did not get on well together. Lubbers put it like this: 'Following the enormous success of reunification, Kohl became a different man. He had steamrollered his way over a few opponents before then, of course, but he had always been quite a good colleague, quite amiable. After

95   Jacques Delors, quoted in Charles Grant, *Delors*, 1994, p. 269.

1990, however, he began towering above himself, he became the first Chancellor of a reunited Germany, he excelled at that, he reveled in it, but he was no longer able to see the other leaders as his colleagues, unless they happened to be president of the United States. He began treating Mitterrand the way Yeltsin later treated Gorbachev, condescendingly, humiliatingly. And when I wanted to do things differently, that irritated him no end.'[96]

After searching around, Kohl found a candidate that was much more to his taste: the Belgian prime minister Jean-Luc Dehaene. He was, like Lubbers, a Christian Democrat. This was an essential requirement, since Jacques Delors had been a socialist. He was also a good friend of Kohl's.

Kohl convinced Mitterrand that Dehaene was the right man for the job and, before Lubbers knew what was happening, the international press had printed the story: Kohl and Mitterrand want Dehaene. Lubbers still didn't give up. He thought he had enough support, having bagged the votes of Spain, Italy and the UK, as well as the Netherlands. He spoke to Kohl one more time. The following exchange took place:

96 Ruud Lubbers, quoted in Geert Mak, *In Europe*, 2007, p. 730.

- But this is undemocratic. Eight of the twelve are for Dehaene. Why won't you accept that? [Kohl]
- I see things differently. Together the four countries who oppose Dehaene's candidacy account for half the population of the EU. Fifty percent of the European population is saying no to this, no matter what you and Mitterrand say. Dehaene and I should both withdraw our candidacy [Lubbers]

Lubbers later recalled: 'Kohl was furious. But that's the way it was, and that's the way it went.'

At the Corfu summit on 25 June 1994, Lubbers was dropped as a candidate. So was Dehaene. John Major, appeasing the Eurosceptics in this party, used his veto to scupper Dehaene's chances. The job of president of the European Commission finally went to a compromise candidate, the Luxembourg prime minister Jacques Santer.

Photo:
Ruud Lubbers of the Netherlands (left) and Jean-Luc Dehaene of Belgium

32

1 January 1995
Austria, Sweden and Finland join the EU

Three countries have good memories of the Corfu Summit. It was on that Greek island that Austria, Sweden and Finland signed the accession treaties that brought them into the European Union.[97] The treaties came into effect on 1 January 1995, bringing the total number of member states to 15.

These three countries were all neutral. They became members – like the Communist countries that joined in 2004 – as a direct result of the fall of the Berlin Wall. Austria had once been at the centre of the vast Hapsburg Empire. Following the collapse of Communism, it immediately saw new opportunities emerging. As early as January 1989, it had put forward an official application for membership. Sweden had been neutral since 1814, while Finland shared a 1,200-kilometre border with the Soviet Union. Both of those countries turned towards the European Union as they watched the Soviet Empire disintegrate.

97   Norway had also negotiated to join but, in a repeat of 1972, voters rejected the bid for membership in a referendum.

Economically speaking, all three countries were members of the European Free Trade Association (EFTA), along with Norway, Iceland and Switzerland. The United Kingdom had also been a member of this loose trade association, which was originally founded as an alternative to the EU but was now losing some of its key member states. The European Union offered a common trade policy, a rudimentary form of foreign and security policy and the prospect of a single currency. For most countries, this seemed in the end more attractive than EFTA's benefits. (The Norwegians and Swiss have chosen to remain outside the EU, but Iceland requested membership in July 2009, following meltdown in their banking sector).

Even before they officially became members, Austria, Sweden and Finland were integrated into the European single market and busily adopting EU legislation. Just like their EFTA partners, they had negotiated a solid agreement with the Twelve establishing a European Economic Area (EEA). This was a concept formulated by Jacques Delors soon after the fall of the Berlin Wall and designed to slow down expansion of the EU. Delors was afraid that the accession of new member states would weaken the Union; he wanted to make the EU stronger, or 'deeper'. The Maastricht Treaty had already taken tentative steps in this direction.

The EEA agreement, which came into force in January 1994, functioned as a sort of 'waiting room'. It was the most far-reaching construction ever devised by the EU for non-members, creating a free trade zone for goods and services as well as free movement of people[98] and capital. It required EFTA countries to incorporate some 4,000 European laws and regulations into their national legislation (including all laws governing the internal market along with European environmental laws and competition rules).

For their part, Austria, Sweden and Finland concluded that, since they were being asked to adopt European legislation, it was in their interests that they had a say in the legislative process. They asked for – and were granted – a voice in the European decision-making machine. This was quite possibly the most important gain they achieved from joining.

Once a country belonged to the EEA, it was only a small step to full EU membership, at least in economic terms. In practical terms, three requirements had to be fulfilled. They had to implement the common external tariff, participate in the common agricultural policy, and prepare for the upcoming economic and monetary union. Austria and Finland were perfectly willing to do that, but Sweden remained attached to its own currency. While Austria and Finland have now adopted the euro, Sweden still refuses to abandon its krona.

On 1 January 1995, the Union welcomed the three small[99] and prosperous member states. From that day on, the Union was more environmentally-aware and more open in its policies. This latter aspect was largely due to Sweden, which had an exemplary reputation with regard to transparent government. But it remained to be seen whether Europe could continue to work efficiently, now that there were 15 countries sitting around the table and many others waiting in the wings.

[98] The EFTA countries belong to the Schengen area, which allows free movement between member states without border controls.

[99] Sweden has a population of 9.2 million, Austria 8.3 million and Finland 5.3 million.

Photo:
The Swedish delegates sign the accession treaty: (left to right) Frank Belfrage, Margaretha af Ugglas, Carl Bildt and Ulf Dinkelspiel

33

Small changes to the treaty at the Amsterdam Summit

100 Timothy Garton Ash, *History of the Present*, 1999, p. 313.

101 The lowest point in the conflict came in July 1995, when Bosnian Serb fighters captured the town of Srebrenica, a United Nations safe haven. An estimated 7,000-8,000 Bosnian Muslim men and boys were taken away and executed in the largest mass murder since the Second World War. The town at the time was under the protection of some 400 Dutch armed peacekeepers, but they failed to prevent the genocide.

102 This traumatic experience led to a much closer defence cooperation between the United Kingdom and France. This was formally agreed in Saint-Malo in 1998 at a meeting between Blair en Chirac.

The writer Timothy Garton Ash was in Amsterdam in 1997 for the Amsterdam Summit. Under the leadership of the Dutch prime minister, Wim Kok, the leaders of the fifteen member states had come together to talk about an 'update' to the Treaty of Maastricht. Garton Ash captured the mood of the moment: '18-20 June. Amsterdam. Just after the European summit, and the whole city is complaining about the disruption to traffic and everyday life. There is no single hint of pride in the Amsterdam Treaty. In fact, I don't think it's ever mentioned.' [100]

There was no evidence at the Amsterdam Summit of the passion that had marked the Maastricht Summit six years earlier. One reason for this was, quite simply, the unfortunate fact that some of the leaders didn't get on with one another. For some reason, the chemistry didn't work between France's Jacques Chirac, Spain's José Maria Aznar and the recently-elected British prime minister Tony Blair. Kohl was still there representing Germany, but he had to hand over power to the social democrat Gerhard Schröder at the end of 1998.

The main question that had to be confronted was whether or not the member states could improve their foreign and security policy. The violence in former Yugoslavia had made this question a particularly urgent one. Despite all their good intentions, the Fifteen had failed to prevent the brutality[101] of the various wars fought from 1991 to 1995 . The violence only came to an end after US bombing missions secured the Dayton Peace Agreement of 1995. This was a humiliating experience for Europe – particularly France and the United Kingdom.[102]

Were any major breakthroughs achieved at the Amsterdam Summit? The answer is no, unless you believe that the creation of a 'High Representative for Common Foreign and Security Policy' represented a major step forward. Javier Solana of Spain, at the time secretary-general of Nato, was widely tipped for the post, which he finally obtained in June 1999. But it was still not at all clear what role the High Representative was in fact meant to play in the world.

The Fifteen made little progress in security and foreign policy, but they did make advances in the fields of police and justice. This was known in EU jargon as the third pillar. An agreement was reached in Amsterdam that moved responsibility for visas, asylum and immigration from the member states to the EU. This meant that the Commission, the European Parliament and the Court of Justice would now be involved in these areas. The summit also saw the incorporation of the Schengen Agreement into the mainstream of EU legislation.[103]

One burning issue remained to be resolved: how was the EU going to adapt its working methods? This was necessary now that it had expanded from the original six to 15 members, and would become even more urgent as it incorporated further member states.

The shift to qualified majority voting wasn't a complete solution. The larger countries – Germany, the United Kingdom, France and Italy – each had ten votes in the Council (while Spain had eight). Meanwhile, small countries each had five or three votes, even though their population was only one quarter of the size (or sometimes much less) of the large countries. With each expansion, the relative weight of the smaller countries became more significant. The large countries were increasingly unhappy with a system which was evolving to a point where they could easily be outvoted. So they wanted a

103 The Schengen Agreement, signed in 1995, allowed residents of EU member states (except for the UK and Ireland) to travel freely within the European Union without border controls. The agreement was originally signed in 1985 in the Luxembourg town of Schengen, near the meeting point of the borders of Germany, France and Luxembourg. The agreement was symbolically signed by Germany, France and the Benelux countries on a river boat in the middle of the River Mosel.

...

Photo:
Setting off on bicycles (a gift from the Amsterdam city council at the Amsterdam Summit: (left to right) Wim Kok of the Netherlands, Tony Blair of Great Britain, José Maria Aznar of Spain and Jean-Luc Dehaene of Belgium (behind)

different system in place before the accession of the Central European states (which, with the exception of Poland, were all small countries).

The preparatory meetings had already shown that the question of voting weight was one which often led to angry exchanges, not only between small and big countries, but also between different small countries. The Netherlands, for example, argued that it should have more votes than Belgium, whose population was significantly smaller.

The Fifteen failed during the Amsterdam Summit to reach an agreement on this issue. The solution that was proposed in the amended treaty simply postponed the decision to a later date.[104] At the end of the summit, the Belgian prime minister, Jean-Luc Dehaene, told the press: 'We construct Europe step by step, and every step forwards is a step in the right direction.'[105] But the Amsterdam Treaty, which was signed in October and came into effect in 1999, was a fairly unimpressive step forwards.

104 The issue was not even resolved in 2000, when the Nice Treaty was signed. It in fact remained undecided until the Lisbon Treaty in 2007.

105 Jean-Luc Dehaene, press conference on 18 June 1999, Amsterdam.

1 January 1999
Economic and monetary union takes off

One date stands out above all others in the history of European integration: 1 January 1999. That was the day when European monetary union came into force and the euro was introduced as an accounting currency in all the countries that had made the required preparations: Belgium, the Netherlands, Luxembourg, Finland, Germany, Ireland, France, Italy, Spain, Portugal and Austria. The exchange rate was set on that day and couldn't be altered. That meant that one euro was equal to 1.95583 German marks, 6.55957 French francs or 0.787564 Irish pounds. The European Central Bank (ECB), an independent body based in Frankfurt, was now in charge of monetary policy and independently set the interest rate levels in the entire eurozone. Its main role was to maintain price stability.

The euro coins and banknotes didn't enter into circulation until 1 January 2002. The national currencies were abolished on that day and banks brought out an enormous quantity of shiny new coins and crisp banknotes. In the meantime, Greece had joined the eurozone in 2001, although no one in those heady days anticipated that this would lead to a major European crisis in 2009 when Greece turned out to have a frightening level of deficit.

The eurozone has subsequently expanded as other member states abandon their national currencies – Slovenia in 2007, Cyprus and Malta in 2008, Slovakia in 2009 and Estonia in 2011. When this book went to press, the eurozone was made up of 17 different countries.[106] The main country to remain outside was, needless to say, the United Kingdom, even though London is the EU's largest financial centre.

The euro is supported by the European Stability and Growth Pact, under which member states are expected to follow a strict budgetary policy. This means that the annual budget deficit must be no higher than three percent of gross domestic product (GDP) and the national debt must be lower than 60 percent of GDP. The Stability and Growth Pact was proposed by Germany and the Netherlands and provided for naming and shaming of offending members who allowed their budgets to drift out of control. In serious cases, fines could be imposed.

106 The finance ministers from the countries that share the euro belong to the eurogroup, which is currently chaired by Jean-Claude Juncker of Luxembourg.

Initially, it seemed as if the Stability and Growth Pact was having the desired effect. Any country that looked as if it was going off the rails would receive a warning letter from the Commission. They would then adapt their policy. But the rules seemed to change in 2004, when Germany (under Schröder) and France (under Chirac) allowed their budget deficit to drift above the three percent ceiling. There was no longer any mention of sanctions or a fine. On the contrary, the rules were relaxed, with the Commission's approval.

The Dutch could hardly believe their eyes.[107] The strict rules governing the Stability Pact had been undermined by Germany – the very country that had worked so hard to introduce it. This seismic shift in Germany's position has made it even more difficult for the eurozone to solve what has become its most pressing problem – how can the member states keep an eye on the other euro economies and what measures can be taken against countries that break the rules?

But no one was thinking about problems like this on 1 January 1999. Ten years after the famous deal between Kohl and Mitterrand (in which Germany got reunification and France got the European currency), the euro had finally become a reality. Economic and monetary union was the high point of European integration, the icing on the cake. The euro would make life easier for European citizens, while businesses would gain enormous benefits at no cost to themselves. In addition, it offered member states a mechanism that would cushion them from financial shocks.

The historian Timothy Garton Ash wrote, 'But few would dissent from the proposition that European monetary union is an unprecedented, high-risk gamble.'[108] Scarcely anyone agreed with this lonely voice crying in the wilderness. Yet there were some good reasons to be cautious. If it was to work, the common currency not only needed a central bank; it also had to include a mechanism to allow automatic fiscal transfers to countries that were experiencing temporary difficulties. It also required a highly mobile labour market. Critics noted that the United States has such a system, but Europe does not. This is a basic weakness in the eurozone which leads to difficulties.

The critics were proved right in 2010 when the Greek economy went into freefall and the debt crisis spread in 2011 to Portugal and Ireland.

107 When the Dutch finance minister Gerrit Zalm called for a fine to be imposed, he was brushed aside by the Germans, who dubbed him an apologist for the Stability Pact. And when Frits Bolkestein expressed his reservations on the issue in a TV interview, he almost lost his job as European Commissioner.

108 Timothy Garton Ash, *History of the Present*, 2004, p. 370.

15 December 2001
The Laeken Declaration

On 15 December 2001, not long after two planes hijacked by Al-Qaeda terrorists flew into the Twin Towers, the Fifteen met at the Belgian royal palace in Laeken, northern Brussels. The meeting was chaired by Guy Verhofstadt, prime minister of Belgium (which held the presidency at the time) and later leader of the liberal faction in the European Parliament.

In the immediate aftermath of the attacks on New York and Washington, Verhofstadt had called the White House to offer support on behalf of the European Union. He did not manage to get through to President Bush: the member of staff who should have connected Verhofstadt to the Oval Office had no idea who was calling.

It was a reality check for Europe. After decades of integration, the leaders of Europe still had no presence on the world stage. The question also arose as to whether the European Union was ready to welcome the many countries that were now seeking membership – the Central European states of Poland, the Czech Republic, Slovakia, Hungary and Slovenia; the former Soviet republics of Estonia, Latvia and Lithuania; the islands of Malta and Cyprus; and the Black Sea countries of Romania and Bulgaria.

One year before the September 11 attacks, the French resort of Nice had been the setting for yet another attempt to reform the way Europe worked. That summit had been a miserable failure. The Treaty of Nice, which was the result, attempted to amend the voting procedure, but was criticised on all sides as a failed compromise. On 15 December, the Fifteen issued the Laeken Declaration.

'Fifty years on, the Union stands at a crossroads, a defining moment in its existence. The unification of Europe is near. The Union is about to expand to bring in more than ten new Member States, predominantly Central and Eastern European, thereby finally closing one of the darkest chapters in European history: the Second World War and the ensuing artificial division of Europe. At long last, Europe is on its way to becoming one big family, without bloodshed, a real transformation clearly calling for a different approach from fifty years ago, when six countries first took the lead.'

'At the same time,' the Declaration continued, 'the Union faces twin challenges, one within and the other beyond its borders. Within the Union, the European institutions must be brought closer to its citizens. Citizens undoubtedly support the Union's broad aims, but they do not always see a connection between those goals and the Union's everyday action. They want the European institutions to be less unwieldy and rigid and, above all, more efficient and open. Many also feel that the Union should involve itself more with their particular concerns, instead of intervening, in every detail, in matters by their nature better left to Member States' and regions' elected representatives. This is even perceived by some as a threat to their identity. More importantly, however, they feel that deals are all too often cut out of their sight and they want better democratic scrutiny.'

The Declaration moved on to consider the global situation: 'Beyond its borders, in turn, the European Union is confronted with a fast-changing, globalised world. Following the fall of the Berlin Wall, it looked briefly as though we would for a long while be living in a stable world order, free from conflict, founded upon human rights. Just a few years later, however, there is no such certainty. The eleventh of September has brought a rude awakening. [...].'

'What amendments should be made to the treaty on the various policies? How, for example, should a more coherent common foreign policy and defence policy be developed? [...] Do we want to adopt a more integrated approach to police and criminal law cooperation? How can economic policy coordination be stepped up? [...] How should the President of the Commission be appointed: by the European Council, by the European Parliament or should he be directly elected by the citizens? Should the role of the European Parliament be strengthened? Should we extend the right of codecision or not? Should the way in which we elect the members of the European Parliament be reviewed? [...]'

Some people in the audience were possibly nodding off by now. But everyone pricked up their ears at the next point. 'Should national parliaments have a role in areas of European action in which the European Parliament has no competence?' This sounded like something new was being proposed.

And so it was. 'The question ultimately arises as to whether this simplification and reorganisation might not lead in the long run to the adoption of a constitutional text. What might the basic features of such a constitution be?'[109]

This was the first time since the launch of the Schuman Plan that the word 'constitution' had been used in the European context. The Laeken Declaration ended with the setting up of a political Convention that would hold public meetings in Brussels and, within a year, come up with a draft document that would form the basis for a possible constitution.

Verhofstadt must have been pleased with himself on that day. He had managed to inject a new vigour into the debate on the future of Europe.[110]

109 The Laeken Declaration on the future of the European Union, 15 December 2001.

110 In his autobiography, Tony Blair relates a conversation with Bush at the Genoa G8 summit in 2001 which suggests that he again failed to recognise Verhofstadt. 'Who is that guy?' asked Bush. 'He is the prime minister of Belgium,' said Blair. 'You got the Belgians running Europe?' Bush asked incredulously. Tony Blair, A Journey, p. 557.

15 January 2003
A deal is reached on a permanent president

In 2002, the Convention was launched, charged with the task of reflecting on Europe's future and drawing up a draft text for a possible constitution. Who were the main figures involved in this ambitious experiment? First and foremost, Valéry Giscard d'Estaing, the man who established the European Council while he was president of France ('Vive le Conseil Européen!' were his words). Giscard d'Estaing was now 76 years old, and he leaped at the chance of fulfilling this new role. The Convention vice-presidents were former Italian prime minister Giuliano Amato, a professor of constitutional law, and former Belgian prime minister Jean-Luc Dehaene, co-author of the Laeken Declaration.

The Convention also included 15 representatives of the heads of state and government of the member states (one from each country), 30 national members of parliament (two from each member state), 16 members of the European Parliament and two representatives from the Commission. The candidate member states also attended the discussions, although they were barred from objecting if a consensus was about to be reached.

The Convention met in the European Parliament building in Brussels. Its sessions were open to the public and all the documents could be consulted. The proceedings and draft treaty can still be consulted online.[111]

One theme dominated the discussions from the outset: foreign policy, or Europe's role in the world. In the beginning, quite a number of participants wanted to shift foreign policy to the Community. This was the position taken by the members of the European Parliament, the Commission, the national members of parliament and the government representatives from the smaller member states.

Iraq, however, showed the fatal weakness in the argument for a European foreign policy. The EU's response to US invasion plans was compromised by internal bickering and division, proving that a common foreign policy, even though several countries wanted it, was never really a serious option. Yet the member states, even those like France and the UK that didn't want to have foreign policy dictated to them, realised that something had to be done. One option was to create a permanent president of the European Council – some-

111 Following the Convention, an intergovernmental conference was held to finalise the details of Europe's constitution, which eventually became the Lisbon Treaty. See: http://european-convention.eu.int

one who could represent the European Union on the world stage.

The situation up until then was that the role of president went to the head of state or government of the country holding the six-month presidency. Under the proposed new system, the president would not have any national mandate and could occupy the post for several years. It was thought that this would give him or her greater authority to speak on behalf of the Fifteen (or, as it would soon be, the Twenty-Seven).[112]

Some countries were from the outset enthusiastic about the idea of a permanent president: France (Chirac and also Giscard d'Estaing[113]), the United Kingdom (Blair) and Spain (Aznar). Others were extremely worried about the proposal. This was especially true of the smaller countries, who were afraid of becoming pawns in the hands of the larger states and preferred to see the Commission given a greater role.[114]

It became evident that Germany's Schröder would have to play a vital role in the process. In the beginning, Germany hesitated, but it eventually reached an agreement with France: Germany would back the idea of a permanent president of the European Council as long as France in return allowed the president of the Commission to be appointed by the European Parliament.[115] The core element of this deal, which was announced to the world on 15 January 2003, was embodied in the Constitutional Treaty as well as the Lisbon Treaty.

This led to the surprise decision at the end of 2009 to appoint the Belgian prime minister Herman van Rompuy as the first permanent president of the European Council. The role of president was to 'at his level and in that capacity, ensure the external representation of the Union on issues concerning its common foreign and security policy'.[116] At the same time, the European Parliament approved the appointment of José Manuel Barroso for a second term as president of the Commission.

The Convention also introduced the idea of a permanent European foreign minister, with his or her own ministry and a foothold in the Commission. This job finally came into existence at the end of 2009 with the appointment of the British politician Cathy Ashton, who at the time was EU Trade Commissioner.

The reader at this point might be baffled. Many other people were, including politicians who had no idea what was happening. Everyone was waiting anxiously for the moment when Europe finally found a single champion to defend its interests.

112 The large countries also wanted to avoid a situation in which, following enlargement, they ended up being represented on the world stage by a tiny member state such as Malta.

113 Giscard d'Estaing originally proposed the creation of a European president who would have his or her own entourage and a wide margin of discretion.

114 The Netherlands under Balkenende was one of the countries that opposed the creation of a permanent president. Belgium, on the other hand, was remarkably swift in reaching a decision to support the concept of a permanent president.

115 Luuk van Middelaar, *De Passage naar Europa*, 2009, p. 289.

116 Treaty on European Union, Article 15.

10 July 2003
One step closer to a European constitution

Valéry Giscard d'Estaing, chairman of the Convention charged with drawing up a draft text for a European constitution, was never one to be put off by a challenge. After the talks had dragged on for longer than anticipated and there was growing doubt about the ultimate success of Europe's constitutional experiment, he placed a porcelain statuette on his desk in the parliament building. Wui-Kei was a tortoise with a dragon's head, he would explain to anyone who asked. It was a patient beast with, so the Chinese said, enormous willpower, so that it always achieved its goal in the end.

On 10 July 2003, the Convention held its final session. Giscard d'Estaing sat down at the table with a smiling Dehaene on his left and a solemn Amato to his right. Finally, he could announce to the world that the project had been a genuine success: all those public meetings and endless discussions had created a constitutional text that would make Europe simpler and also more democratic.

After he had delivered his speech, Giscard d'Estaing made a theatrical disappearance under his desk. Then, in front of the hastily-assembled press, he emerged again clutching a few lettuce leaves, and, grinning broadly, proceeded to feed them to Wui-Kei. With Europe's draft constitution completed, Giscard's ornamental tortoise had well and truly earned its lettuce leaves. The following day, photographs of Giscard d'Estaing and his tortoise were in all the newspapers.

What, then, were the main points in the draft text that Giscard d'Estaing presented to the world on 10 July 2003?

- The European Council – where heads of state and government reach decisions – gets a permanent president;
- The new post of European foreign minister is created. He or she reports to the member states while at the same time sitting in the European Commission. The foreign minister would be supported by a newly-created diplomatic service known as the European External Action Service staffed by diplomats drawn from the member states and civil servants from the Commission;

117 The Lisbon Treaty
states that this rule
will come into force
on 1 November
2014.

118 The Charter of
Fundamental Rights
covers all civil,
political, economic
and social rights
enjoyed by Euro-
pean citizens and
all other people
present in the terri-
tory of the European
Union. It was formu-
lated by an ad hoc
Convention made
up of 62 members:
15 representatives
of the heads of state
and government,
one representative
of the Commission,
16 representatives
of the European
Parliament and 30
representatives of
the national parlia-
ments.

- Responsibility for justice and home affairs (the former 'third pillar') shifts from the national to the European level. The aim here was to deal more effectively with illegal immigration, cross-border crime, human trafficking and the smuggling of weapons and drugs;
- Qualified majority voting was to be the rule in meetings of the Council of Ministers. The majority was precisely defined: a decision could be passed with the support of at least 55 percent of member states representing in total 65 percent of the population of Europe;[117]
- The European Parliament gains the power of codecision with the Council of Ministers in more than 40 new areas, including agriculture, energy, security, immigration, justice and home affairs. The members of the European Parliament would also be given a greater role in approving the budget of the European Union; they also gained the right to elect the president of the Commission;
- National parliaments would be more closely involved in the legislative process, and would gain the right to challenge legislation at an early stage in the process;
- European citizens could call on the Commission to draw up draft legislation on a particular subject, if they could obtain more than one million signatures from a 'significant' number of member states;
- The Charter of Fundamental Rights – which had existed since 2000 although scarcely anyone had heard of it – was incorporated into the constitution, which made it legally binding.[118]

Photo:
Valéry Giscard d'Estaing
with his Chinese porce-
lain tortoise Wui-Kei

The European Union gained a national anthem, a flag, a motto and an official Europe Day (9 May). In addition, the legislators made a conscious effort to write in plain language, using words like 'minister' and 'law'. After all that, it is hardly surprising that Giscard d'Estaing, Amato and Dehaene looked so happy when, at the end of the Convention, they shook each other by the hand. They of course had no idea of the painful setbacks that lay ahead for the European constitution.

38

1 May 2004
The big bang: from 15 to 25 member states in one day

On 1 May 2004, ten new countries became members of the European Union. From that day, 25 chairs would be needed to seat each country at the negotiating table. The new members had extremely diverse histories and identities:

- Poland (population 38.5 million), a country that suffered enormously in the Second World War and whose Solidarnosc trade union finally brought the Communist government to its knees;
- Czech Republic (population 10.2 million), the country of Vaclav Havel, Franz Kafka and Milan Kundera;
- Hungary (population 9.9 million), a country that shared a Hapsburg past with Austria and was once much larger;
- Slovakia (population 5.4 million), whose capital Bratislava was just one hour's drive from Vienna;
- Estonia, Latvia and Lithuania (1.3 million, 2.2 million and 3.6 million respectively), the three Baltic states, which bravely broke away from the Soviet Union after the fall of the Berlin Wall;
- Slovenia (population 2 million), a country that largely escaped the violence that engulfed much of former Yugoslavia;
- The Mediterranean islands of Cyprus, the birthplace of the Greek goddess Aphrodite, and Malta, which only gained independence from the United Kingdom in 1964 (793,000 and 404,000 inhabitants respectively).

Each of the ten countries was granted a Commissioner and directly-elected representatives in the European Parliament – quite a special experience for the eight countries who shared a repressive Communist past. Poland was by far the largest of the new states; with a population of 38.5 million, it was on a level with Spain, and almost four times larger than, for instance, Belgium. The countries that formerly belonged to the Soviet bloc had done everything possible to become members of the European Union. As early as the Velvet Revolutions of 1989, the slogan 'Return to Europe' had been a popular rallying call. To facilitate their membership applications, these countries had enacted constitutions, constructed stable legal systems and recognised the rights of minorities. They had also implemented shock therapies to turn themselves into market economies, a process that had introduced their citizens to the experience of unemployment for the first time in many decades. In addition, these former Soviet satellites had opened their markets to European products and services, and promised at some point in the future to replace their national currencies with the euro. They had moreover incorporated the full body of European law into their national legislation and concluded weighty agreements that laid down how and when they would transform their agricultural sector to conform to the European common agricultural policy.

The accession treaties were signed by all the parties involved and adopted in the different countries with enormous popular enthusiasm. On 1 May 2004, the treaties officially entered into effect, and ten brightly-decorated hot-air balloons took off into the sky from the Cinquantenaire Park in Brussels. People stopped to stare at the spectacle. The look on their faces was one of amazement.

The European Union changed on that one day in May more than most people had anticipated. The eastern border of the Union shifted in one huge leap from the Oder and Neisse line to the rivers Boeg and Oezj. The geographical centre was no longer located in a field somewhere between France and Germany, but much further east, close to Berlin (where Chancellor Schröder had taken up residence in the shiny new glass Kanzleramt). The big worry was that this 'big bang' would lead to paralysis in the Union. This didn't happen, despite the fact that the Lisbon Treaty was still a long way from being ratified. With its expansion to the east, the European Union has grown to some 500 million inhabitants, or seven percent of the world population, collectively responsible for generating 22 percent of the world's wealth.[119] The challenge that Europeans now face is how to promote and protect their values and interests in a world that is rapidly changing. What do Europeans want? What story do they want to tell the world?

119 This figure includes the populations of Romania and Bulgaria, who joined the EU in 2007.

39

18 June 2004

Blair blocks Verhofstadt as Commission president

According to those who know about this sort of thing, the position of president of the European Commission is not a dream job. 'Presidents,' wrote Dutch political commentator Derk-Jan Eppink, 'very soon become exhausted, suffer from sleepless nights, put on too much weight, raise their cholesterol to dangerous levels and can count on being criticised constantly.'[120]

'Monsieur le président' can lord it over people on the 13th floor of the Berlaymont, but outside the Commission they see their power ebb away, particularly now that the permanent president of the European Council is slowly but surely taking over their territory. Within the Commission the president is a person of some substance but in the outside world he is the first to be criticised by government leaders and the media when things go wrong. The job of leading the European Commission in the current climate is a lonely one.

Even so, Guy Verhofstadt had set his heart on this job in 2004. He was spurred on by the then French President Jacques Chirac who asked him at a meeting in the Elysée whether he might be available to succeed Romano Prodi at the end of 2004. 'Surtout, cher Guy, ne faites rien,' ('Above all, dear Guy, don't do anything'), Chirac advised. 'Gerhard [Schröder] and I will take care of it.'

Supported by France and Germany, it really did look as if Belgium was going to provide the next president of the European Commission. It's hard not to forget just how pleased Verhofstadt looked when he announced his candidacy on a bright spring day in 2004. He had long cherished the dream of giving the European Union a more prominent role in the world, and his head was bursting with ideas that would make him into a sort of liberal version of Jacques Delors.

So what went wrong during the Brussels Summit of June 18, 2004? By then Verhofstadt and his advisers had already jetted across Europe, and were convinced that there was a consensus on appointing Verhofstadt as president.

Rewind to the beginning of 2003, when the American decision to invade Iraq left Europe hopelessly divided. Some leaders (including Britain's Blair, Italy's Berlusconi, Spain's Aznar and Portugal's Barroso) supported US President Bush publicly from the outset. On the other hand, France, Germany and Belgium were firmly opposed to the White House plans.

120 Derk-Jan Eppink, *Europese Mandarijnen*, 2007, p. 189.

On 20 March 2003, untroubled by European opposition, America invaded Iraq. Baghdad fell on April 9. Verhofstadt responded with an initiative that has gone down in history as the 'praline summit'. He proposed the creation of a European army as a counterweight to Nato forces. Verhofstadt invited Chirac, Schröder and Luxembourg's Junker to Brussels to talk about the different options. The praline summit was a flop. The pro-American member states – with the UK at the head of the pack – were categorically opposed to the Belgian prime minister's initiative.

Verhofstadt's presidential bid met with similar strong opposition. It is important to remember at this point that the Christian Democrats swept to victory in the European elections in 2004, and that Angela Merkel's German Christian Democrats were opposed to the idea of Verhofstadt, a liberal democrat, at the head of the Commission. The tide had turned against Verhofstadt.

On 18 June 2004, Tony Blair used his veto to exclude Guy Verhofstadt from running for president. Silvio Berlusconi joined him. Other countries followed, including several of the new East European countries that had only recently joined the European Union and wanted to show their teeth. The same evening, a new president emerged unexpectedly. It was José Manuel Barroso, prime minister of Portugal, a Christian Democrat who was instinctively less federalist than Guy Verhofstadt.

At the end of the day, the heads of state and government leaders flew home to their capitals. The Belgian prime minister remained seated at the conference table. When he emerged into the daylight, he looked purposeful. But, if you looked closely, you could see that the eyes behind his glasses were dark.

Photo:
Tony Blair (left) and Guy Verhofstadt

40 | *21 September 2004*
The Services Directive comes under fire

On 21 September 2004, the European Commissioner for the Internal Market, Frits Bolkestein, made a speech in Brussels on the need to open up Europe's services sector to cross-border competition. 'The internal market is one of the pillars of our prosperity, it is the basis of our social structure,' the Dutch Commissioner told his audience of Flemish business leaders. 'Belgium and the Netherlands are small countries. Our home market is too small. Entrepreneurs in the Low Countries depend on exports; they depend on the European market of 450 million consumers. An entrepreneur from West Flanders or Limburg needs to export goods and services to Poland, Greece or Portugal. [...]'

He went on, 'The European Union needs not only a free market in goods, but also services, labour and capital. The Commission has produced a services directive to allow professionals to work freely in the European Union and offer their services in any member state. The services sector represents the lion's share of economic activity and so provides much of the impetus. The directive has been attacked, mainly by the left. In Belgium it has become known as the Bolkestein directive. That is of course an honour, but socialists and greens spit out my name as if I am the Abominable Snowman. The Belgian trade unions have seen fit to rename the proposal the Frankenstein directive. [...]'

'Is it socially regressive to grant a sick person the right to seek medical assistance in a neighbouring country?' he asked. 'Ask that to patients who are confronted with long waiting lists. Is it socially regressive if an architect sets up his firm in another European country and helps to create new jobs in the building industry? Ask that to the millions of unemployed who are looking for a job.'[121]

In pursuit of his aims, Bolkestein proposed a directive on 'mutual recognition' that allowed someone who was qualified as a service provider in one EU member state to offer that service across the whole European market. The free movement of goods and capital had already been achieved under Delors using the same basic principle. But computer specialists, architects, estate agents or travel agents were still confronted with endless red-tape when

121 Frits Bolkestein, speech to Vlaams Economisch Verbond, the Flanders Chamber of Commerce and Industry, on 21 September 2004.

they tried to work outside their own country – they needed to obtain permits, register with the authorities, and so on. The result was that European unity remained an empty promise for these people. The Dutchman Derk-Jan Eppink, who was closely involved in the services directive,[122] saw Bolkestein's plan as a step in the right direction.

'The legal service gave the green light to the measure because the Commission was legally obliged under the Treaties to complete the internal market. The other Commissioners raised no objections. Nor did anyone object at the meeting of heads of cabinet or the Commissioners' weekly meeting. Everyone agreed, full stop. For an EU mandarin, this was a textbook example of legislation.'[123]

But that was before the member states (meeting in the Council of Ministers) and the European Parliament became involved. They were of course the bodies that would determine the final shape of the proposed law when (or if) it entered the national statute books. This is where Bolkestein's plan began to fall apart. The resistance began in Belgium, where the socialist trade unions (particularly in French-speaking Wallonia) argued that the market would become flooded with workers, such as Poles, who would undercut Belgian workers by accepting Polish wages (this was untrue). They were also afraid that all public services would be forced to liberalise (which was again untrue). The trade union demonstrations started soon after this. By the time Frits Bolkestein was due to defend his services directive in Brussels on 21 September 2004, the chances of success were almost nil.

122 Eppink was employed in Bolkestein's cabinet at the time; he is now a member of the European Parliament.

123 Derk-Jan Eppink, *Europese Mandarijnen*, 2007, p. 246.

Photo:
An estimated 50,000 people marched through Brussels in protest at the Bolkestein directive

124 In his book *Europese Mandarijnen*, Eppink noted the 'remarkable' voting behaviour of the Belgian Philippe Busquin: as a member of the Commission he was in favour of the Bolkestein directive, but as a member of the European Parliament he voted against.

125 In 'Directive 2006/123/EC of the European Parliament and of the Council on services in the internal market', no mention was made of 'mutual recognition'. Furthermore, entire sectors were excluded from the list of services.

In November 2004, the Barroso Commission took over, and the Irishman Charlie McCreevy replaced Bolkestein. In France, where the no-campaign against the European constitution was gathering momentum, the people took to the streets in protest. The services directive was seen as a symbol of a socially regressive Europe and came under increasing fire. Members of the European Parliament who had initially backed the Commission were now distancing themselves from the proposal.[124] McCreevy offered little or no support to Bolkestein's text. Once government ministers realised that backing the idea of free movement of services was not going to win them any votes, the services directive was effectively dead in the water.

The directive that finally emerged was nothing like the plan put forward by Frits Bolkestein.[125] This is a pity, say economists, since the free movement of services would have helped Europe weather the financial crisis that engulfed the global economy in 2008.

29 May 2005
France kills off the European constitution

In 2003, the Convention completed its work with a draft treaty that gave Europe its first constitution. The document was remarkably clearly drafted by the Convention, but in the end wasn't adopted as it stood by the 25 member states. The treaty text they finally approved in June 2004 reflected the position of the Central European countries where, after several decades of Soviet rule, people were reluctant to surrender their sovereignty once again. Poland, for example, joined the United Kingdom in obtaining an opt-out from the Charter of Fundamental Rights. Plans to give the Commission more power in monitoring budgets were also scrapped. The emphasis thus shifted from the European institutions (Commission, Parliament, Court of Justice) to the member states. But the main principles of the 'Treaty establishing a constitution for Europe' remained intact.

On 29 October 2004, the television news showed Europe's heads of state and government climbing the steps of the Capitol in Rome. They entered the breathtakingly beautiful Sala degli Orazi e Curiazi of the Palazzo dei Conservatori, where the Six had sat to sign the Treaty of Rome in 1957. The hall was decorated with European flags for the occasion, while Beethoven's Ode to Joy, the official European anthem, was played on loudspeakers.

President Chirac of France looked almost regal as he entered the hall, as if he wanted to show that France had played an essential role in this historic moment. Tony Blair grinned somewhat uneasily at the cameras. The host, Silvio Berlusconi, made sure that everyone noticed as he wiped away a tear. At the front of the room, there was a beautifully-bound version of the treaty, with a wooden box next to it containing 25 pens. After the last person had signed the treaty, the room broke out in resounding applause. All 25 leaders had signed the constitution that would make the European Union more democratic, transparent and efficient. The European citizen had every reason to be happy.

But happy European citizens turned out to be thin on the ground. They certainly weren't to be found in France, where on Sunday 29 May 2005 the French people gave an overwhelming non in a referendum held by the Chirac government to approve the treaty, with 55 percent of voters against it.

France, the country that had given Europe the founding fathers of Schuman and Monnet, had rejected the European constitution. This blow was far more severe than any blow that Mrs Thatcher dealt with her famous handbag. And it got worse. Three days later, the Dutch voted 'nee' in a similar referendum, with even more of the electorate against the constitution (61.6 percent).

Europe's presidents and prime ministers could hardly believe their eyes. Jacques Chirac, deeply upset by the outcome, sent his government packing. The Dutch prime minister Jan-Peter Balkenende took a deep breath and declared that the European constitution was dead.[126] Tony Blair could hardly conceal his relief, since this meant that he would not have to hold a referendum.

Why, then, did the voters turn against the European constitution? How did Chirac and the other leaders fail to convince voters of the bright future that lay ahead? These are questions that still haven't been fully answered.

The conclusion which the European leaders drew was that the approach they had taken was far too open. They had used terms like 'Convention', 'constitution' and 'European minister of foreign affairs'. The people at home saw this as a threat, and concluded that their country would soon be swallowed up by Europe.

The leaders announced a period for 'reflection'. That meant: a period of waiting until a new French president was elected. They then produced the Lisbon Treaty to replace the constitution. The content was virtually the same, but it was couched in difficult language. The European documents were once again, as in the old days, almost unreadable. And now we know why. It's because the government leaders in 2005 decided that treaties that could be understood would be seen by the citizens as a threat. The age of clarity had passed.

126 This was unusually tough language for Balkenende. But the 'No' that stopped Europe in its tracks came from France. If the Dutch had stood alone against the treaty, then the Netherlands would almost certainly have been forced to hold a second referendum, as happened with Denmark in 2007 and Ireland in 2008.

Photo:
Jacques Chirac addresses the French nation on television

1 January 2007
Romania and Bulgaria join the EU

On 1 January 2007, some 18 months after the French and Dutch voted down the European constitution, two states bordering the Black Sea joined the EU – Romania with a population of 22.5 million and Bulgaria with 7.3 million people. As with the ten countries that had joined in 2004, the two new member states had spent several years transforming themselves into stable and democratic free market economies in line with the EU model. The accession of Romania and Bulgaria brought the total number of member states on New Year's Day to 27. No one could possibly have imagined such a number before the collapse of the Soviet Union.

The Romanians and Bulgarians celebrated this historic moment with fireworks and champagne. In the old member states, however, the mood was far more cautious. The reason that the French and Dutch had voted no to the constitution was that they felt that the EU had expanded too quickly. It had become 'too big' and 'too much' The disturbing pictures and stories emanating from the new countries (involving corruption, organised crime and badly-run orphanages) suggested that the European Commission, which was meant to determine whether a country was ready for membership, had failed in its role. As a result, the members decided to avoid any future 'big bang' expansion. Any country that wants to join the EU in future will be assessed on its own merits according to rigorous criteria.[127]

127 The Copenhagen criteria, as they are known, on membership are now enshrined in the Lisbon Treaty.

In February 2010, the Czech Stefan Füle was appointed European Commissioner in charge of enlargement for the next five years. It was not going to be an easy job. Virtually no one was disputing that the new Balkan countries, which had been born out of so much bloodshed and pain, would join the EU at some time in the future. The only question was how quickly this process would happen.

Croatia is currently the most advanced, with the accession negotiations now almost at an end. Other countries are still waiting in line, having been promised membership at some point – Macedonia (which Greece insists should be called the Former Yugoslav Republic of Macedonia, to avoid confusion with the Greek region of Macedonia), Albania, Bosnia-Herzegovina, Serbia, Montenegro and Kosovo. All of them are small states or even statelets that at some point will have to learn to trust one another again.

128 The first stage is a special free trade agreement known as the Stability and Association Agreement, after which the country is granted the status of candidate member state; the real accession process can only begin once that has happened.

129 The Netherlands and Belgium blocked for a long time the Stability and Accession Agreement with Serbia on the grounds that the country was failing in their opinion to cooperate fully with the Yugoslavia Tribunal.

130 In 1963, Turkey signed an 'association agreement' with the then European Economic Community. Known as the Ankara Agreement, this envisaged full membership, for which Turkey formally applied in 1987. Iceland has also applied to join the European Union. See ec.europa.eu/enlargement for the latest developments.

The road to membership is a long process which is divided into distinct stages.[128] The Netherlands and Belgium have a reputation for being ruthlessly severe in vetting this process.[129] But Italy, France and Germany can also apply the brakes when needed. In the case of the newer member states, however, the faster it happens the better. The United Kingdom is also in favour of rapid expansion, although it is no secret that this is because the UK wants the EU to be substantially weakened.

The future of Turkey is even more controversial. This is a secular Muslim state with 77 million inhabitants, a dynamic economy and a strategically vital location at the crossroads of the Balkans, the Black Sea, the Caucasus and the Middle East. Turkey, which has long enjoyed a customs union with the European Union, was accepted as a candidate member state in 1999. Concrete negotiations on accession began in 2005 and proceeded according to 'chapters', with each chapter covering a specific policy area.

Turkey has already implemented a long list of reforms, including extending more rights to the Kurds and strengthening women's rights. But there are still major hurdles that stand in the way of progress. With its population of 77 million (predicted to rise to 100 million by 2050), Turkey would be the second-largest EU member state, after Germany (82 million) and ahead of France (64.3 million) and Great Britain (61.7 million). The influx of a large Muslim population would profoundly alter the European Union. Leaders such as Nicolas Sarkozy of France and Angela Merkel of Germany have made no secret of the fact that they would prefer Turkey not to join. Some two-thirds of Germans and French support the view that Turkey should be kept out of the EU.

To add to the problem, the question of Cyprus remains unresolved. Turkey continues to occupy part of the island and refuses to allow Cypriot ships to enter the ports. It might be that Turkey's luck changes in the future. But will the Turks themselves still want to throw in their lot with Europe?[130]

22 June 2007

Brussels Summit lays down the foundations for the Lisbon Treaty

The Lisbon Treaty came into existence in Brussels. The driving force behind it was Angela Merkel, Germany's first female Chancellor. Merkel was elected at the end of 2005 and almost immediately hung a portrait of Konrad Adenauer in her Berlin office. She wanted to put Europe back on its feet after the rejection of the constitution.

She took over the presidency of the European Union in January 2007. In May of that year, France had a new president – Nicolas Sarkozy. Merkel seized her opportunity. As the new president, she held talks with Sarkozy, Britain's Blair (who had announced his resignation as prime minister), Poland's Kaczynski and Spain's Zapatero, along with other EU leaders and Commission president Barroso. On 22 June 2007, she invited them to sit down at the large round table in the Justus Lipsius building in Brussels.

On the morning of 27 June, Merkel – who had grown up behind the Iron Curtain – explained the results of the summit in a speech to the European Parliament. She seemed relieved as she reminded the world that: 'None of this – neither peace nor freedom, neither democracy nor the rule of law – can be taken for granted. It must all be strengthened and defended again and again. Standstill actually means a step backwards. Confidence takes decades to build up. But it can be shattered overnight – yes, overnight. [...] European integration has to be striven for and consolidated time and again.'

She continued: 'That is why I am very thankful that we were able to do exactly that with the most recent EU Council. We set the course for a new common basis for the European Union. We ended the standstill. When it came down to it, we did not disappoint confidence. We avoided a rift. To put it simply: what was achieved on Saturday night has given Europe a new, shared energy.'

'I have no wish today to rake over the draining negotiations of the last few weeks and months,' Merkel said. 'We all remember all too well that even the starting position was difficult: on one side, those Member States which fully supported and had already ratified the Constitutional Treaty, and, on the other, those which were demanding substantial changes in response to criticism from their populations.'

131 Angela Merkel, speech to the European Parliament on 27 June 2007.

132 At the end of the day, national parliaments were given new powers to sound the alarm bell in the case of EU legislation that was seen as inappropriate. If enough national parliaments lodged an objection within eight weeks on the grounds that a draft Commission law was not a matter for EU legislation, then the proposal would be sent back to the Commission to be reconsidered.

'Let's not pretend. There was always a danger, namely the danger that the paralysis and the risk of division would persist. Of course it would not have been the end of Europe if the EU Council had not succeeded in getting the desired outcome, but it would undoubtedly have had almost indescribable repercussions. [...]

The agreement reached in Brussels enables us to retain the substance of the Constitutional Treaty. [...] With the Reform Treaty we are taking account of citizens' fears of an alleged 'European superstate', of surrendering too much of the nation-states' identities. I do not share this fear, but I had to respect it. And I did respect it. That is why we decided to refrain from laying down state-like symbols and designations in the Reform Treaty.

The Reform Treaty contains major advances for the European Union's capacity to act. Indeed, in some areas we even went further than in the Constitutional Treaty. Climate protection and energy solidarity were included; the national parliaments will be even more closely involved in shaping national policy on Europe; there will be an even clearer delimitation of competences between the EU and the Member States; and the conditions for enhanced cooperation, particularly on justice and home affairs, were made easier. [...]'

'There is an African saying,' she concluded. 'If you want to move forward fast, then go alone. If you want to go far, go together.'[131]

A smile crossed her face and she shook her head slightly. She was possibly thinking of Balkenende and Verhofstadt. They had almost come to blows at three o'clock in the morning. Balkenende wanted the national parliaments to be directly involved in European legislation. Verhofstadt argued that this put the European project in danger. Merkel had calmed them down like a mother dealing with two squabbling children.[132]

Photo:
Angela Merkel was pleased with the outcome of the Brussels Summit

17 September 2007
European Commission versus Microsoft: 1-0

If there was a prize awarded for bravery, it would without a shadow of doubt go to Neelie Kroes, the current vice-president of the Commission and, up until recently, European Competition Commissioner. The Dutch Commissioner never tired of explaining how she saw her role. 'The European economy is a football match, and my role is to be the referee,' she once wrote. 'Together with the other Commissioners, I set the rules of the game and ensure the teams play by the rules. We ensure that the game is fair, and that there are penalties for people and companies that break the rules and spoil the game for others.'

The appointment of Kroes as Competition Commissioner in 2004 was greeted with suspicion by the members of the European Parliament. Here was a woman who had sat on the boards of several companies. Could she be trusted to be impartial? And would she be able to show the necessary resolve in dealing with companies that had broken the rules (by exploiting their dominant position in the market or forming secret cartels) and in so doing had damaged the interests of consumers (by charging high prices or offering less choice)? 'I'm no kitten,'[133] she once joked in response to her critics.

133 Neelie Kroes, quoted in *Elsevier*, 11 August 2007, p. 48.

One person who was probably rubbing his hands with glee at this point was Microsoft's CEO Steve Balmer. His company had just been hit with a record fine of €497 million for breaking European anti-trust rules. After Kroes took over from the tough Italian Competition Commissioner Mario Monti, Balmer confidently assumed that he wouldn't have to pay the fine after all. He was sure that his lawyers would get him off the hook. But the Dutch Commissioner saw things differently. She imposed a further fine of €280 million because Microsoft had ignored the earlier ruling (the Commission wanted Microsoft to release part of its software protocols and give consumers the possibility of buying the Microsoft operating system without it being bundled with Windows Media Player).

On 17 September 2007, the European Court of First Instance ruled in favour of Kroes on all points. The US software giant was not only forced to pay the fine that had been imposed, but also had to disclose a large part of its software protocols and launch a version of Windows stripped of Media Player.

134 Neelie Kroes, 17
     September 2007.
     You might want
     to know what
     happened to all
     that money that
     Microsoft paid to
     the Commission:
     it was moved from a
     blocked account to
     the EU coffers after
     the Court decision.
     The fines levied by
     the European Com-
     mission are used to
     reduce the contri-
     butions made by the
     27 member states to
     the budget.

135 Neelie Kroes, 27
     September 2007.

136 Noted in Le Canard
     Enchaîné in January
     2010.

'The Court has upheld in full a historic Commission decision to provide consumers with greater choice in the software market,' announced Kroes with a steely stare. 'This creates an important precedent with regard to the obligations of dominant companies to allow competition, particularly in the high-tech industry.'[134] Five months after this decision, Kroes slapped another fine on Microsoft – this time €889 million. 'We have been mild,'[135] she said.

The French president Nicolas Sarkozy, among others, wasn't happy. 'Kroes has no more than two brain cells,'[136] he said during a cabinet meeting. When the global financial and economic crisis erupted in 2008, the emphasis shifted to the second of the main tasks of the Competition Commissioner: intervening in cases where there is a suspicion of illegal state aid. Some forms of state aid are permitted under the European treaty, but there are strict rules governing it. In essence these prevent the member states indulging in an orgy of state aid and hence unfair competition. As a result, a number of key players felt the full weight of Kroes' tough regime. First and foremost were the banks that were being bailed out with government money to prevent them going bust (including a number of banks in her own country), followed by the car manufacturers (Renault and Opel), where national governments had helped them survive the slump in demand by pumping in taxpayers' money. The French president was being scrutinised more closely than he liked; he saw Kroes as nothing more than a troublemaker. But the minister president of Flanders, who was fighting for the future of the Opel Antwerp factory, saw her as an ally.

Photo:
Neelie Kroes at a press
conference in Brussels
on 17 September 2007

Kroes summed it all up as follows: 'Leadership does not involve stealing jobs in neighbouring countries. If you have received support, you are obliged to make cuts, pay back the money and produce a sustainable business model. And yes, this hurts a little. But it doesn't help to moan. Otherwise, it isn't fair to those who haven't received any support.'[137]

How did she deal with Sarkozy? In the end, it was with a smile. The Spaniard Joaquin Almunia was due to take over the competition portfolio while she moved on to become Commissioner for the Digital Agenda. On her last day as Competitition Commissioner, she retorted: 'Two brain cells? Then I still have 100 percent more than he does.'[138]

It is likely that Europe can expect more of the same from 'Steely Neelie', now that she is involved in the digital world.

137 Neelie Kroes, quoted in *Elsevier*, 5 December 2009.

138 Neelie Kroes, quoted in *Handelsblatt*, 8 February 2010.

45

13 December 2007
The Lisbon Treaty is signed

Europe's constitution was ceremoniously signed on the Capitoline Hill in Rome – and then roundly rejected by the public. The Lisbon Treaty, on the other hand, was quietly signed in a monastery – and finally approved by the people.

On 13 December 2007, the European prime ministers and presidents gathered in the Mosteiro dos Jeronimos in Lisbon, where the Portuguese explorer Vasco da Gama lies buried, and took out their pens to sign the treaty. Gordon Brown, who had replaced Tony Blair as the United Kingdom's prime minister, arrived late. Some say it was deliberate. The press had already gone by the time he came around to signing, allegedly because he didn't want any photographs in the newspapers showing him signing the treaty. The British were still very touchy about the idea of their prime minister signing away their sovereignty.

The Lisbon Treaty, which entered into force on 1 December 2009,[139] is nothing less than the Bible of European cooperation. It contains 359 pages of dense legal text and can be consulted online at the website *www.consilium. europa.eu*. But what does this document, this stealth constitution, mean for the citizens of Europe? What new ground rules did it introduce?

- For anyone who wants to understand the European Union, it is no longer enough to look at the work of the Commission, the Council and the European Parliament. The table in the Justus Lipsius building in Brussels where the elected leaders gather regularly for meetings, the European Council in other words, has become much more important. Under the Lisbon Treaty, the table is presided over for the first time by a permanent host, who doesn't vanish with a change of government. That position is currently occupied by the Belgian Herman van Rompuy. The permanent president remains in office for at least two and a half years, with the possibility of remaining in place for up to five years. He gets to know his colleagues well and plays an important role in reconciling their different points of view;

- In relations with the external world, the changes introduced by Lisbon have so far caused a certain degree of confusion. Take the question of who would sit next to US president Obama at the planned EU-US summit in May 2010. Would it be the Commission president Barroso, per-

[139] The Irish voted against the Lisbon Treaty in a first referendum (June 2008), but approved it in a second referendum (October 2009). In France and the Netherlands, no further referendums were organised and the national parliaments ratified the treaty, as did the other member states.

manent president of the European Council Van Rompuy or Zapatero, the prime minister of Spain and rotating president of the European Union?[140] It turned out to be none of the above, since Obama called off the meeting on the grounds that he had better things to do with his time. It is also unclear at this point how far Europe's new foreign minister, Catherine Ashton, can speak in the name of Europe. All we know is that she is the EU's 'High Representative for Foreign Affairs and Security Policy', as well as Commission vice-president – a dual role designed to integrate 'soft' trade and aid policy tools into a coherent EU policy. She heads a newly-created 'diplomatic corps': the European External Action Service (EEAS);

- Problems such as cross-border crime and illegal immigration will be easier for the police and judicial system to tackle, because the national veto has in principle been abolished. Decisions can now generally be reached on the basis of qualified majority voting, although there are some limited exceptions to the rule.[141] As of 2014, a legislative proposal put forward by the Commission will be passed by the Council if it has the support of 55 percent of the member states accounting for 65 percent of the EU's population. The transition period until this comes into force in 2014 is governed by special regulations;
- The European Parliament will be in the news a lot more often in future. The Parliament is now on an equal footing with the Council in the EU decision-making process. In addition, European parliamentarians were granted codecision powers in approving Europe's agricultural budget. They also gained the right to choose the president of the Commission;
- The Charter of Fundamental Rights of the European Union becomes legally-binding for the first time.[142] The treaty also defines the values on which the Union is based: respect for human dignity, freedom, democracy, equality, the rule of law, respect for human rights (including the rights of minorities), pluralism, non-discrimination, tolerance, justice, solidarity and equality of the sexes. All the member states are required to respect these fundamental values;
- The treaty also provides each citizen with a direct line to the Commission. If an individual can join forces on a particular issue with citizens from a 'significant number' of member states and gather one million signatures, the Commission is required to produce a proposal for legislation on that subject. Equally, members of national parliaments can join up with colleagues from other countries to raise the alarm if they believe that the Commission is moving too fast in a particular area.

All in all, a large part of the Convention was imported directly into the Lisbon Treaty. Europe may still not have a constitution, but it has an instrument that is almost as powerful.

140 The function of permanent president only applies to the European Council. The ordinary Councils of Ministers are still organised on a rotating basis. Hungary holds the presidency from January to June 2011, followed by Poland in the second half of the year.

141 The veto still applies in decisions involving defence, tax, family law, criminal measures and expansion of the Union.

142 The UK, Poland and the Czech Republic were granted opt-outs.

46

23 January 2008

Barroso presents an ambitious plan on energy and climate change

The Commission president, José Manuel Barroso, is not someone you would describe as a committed Green. He is not like the Danish Commissioner for Climate Action, Connie Hedegaard, who often sets off for her office in Brussels' Berlaymont building by bicycle. Yet, despite his lukewarm position, Barroso launched a package of legislation on climate change on 23 January 2008 that was seen by the press as being every bit as ambitious and far-reaching as the introduction of the euro and EU enlargement.

Barroso had been trying for years to make the citizen more involved in Europe. In his speech to the press, he said: 'The work of the European Union is sometimes seen as rather technical. It is seen as cut off from daily concerns; interesting to specialists, but not relevant to people's everyday lives. The action we are discussing today proves this theory wrong. The struggle against climate change and the quest for secure, sustainable and competitive energy touches on every European, every day.'[143]

143 José Manuel Barroso, '20 20 by 2020: Europe's climate change opportunity', speech to the European Parliament, 23 January 2008.

Europe had long been aware of the threat of climate change, partly through the campaigning work of Al Gore in the United States and the United Nations (in particular the Intergovernmental Panel on Climate Change, IPCC). Europe became convinced that the environmentalists were right – human beings are responsible for global warming and that this is likely to lead to massive problems worldwide that can best be solved by international cooperation.

This was Europe's chance, according to Barroso and most of the member states, to achieve something positive, after the humiliating defeat of the constitution. If Europe could lead the world in setting ambitious and binding rules, went the reasoning, then it would set an inspiring example that other world powers would undoubtedly decide to follow.

Barroso announced the proposals on 23 January 2008 and they were agreed in record time by the Council (Environment Ministers) and Parliament:

- A 20 percent cut in EU greenhouse gas emissions by 2020 (based on 1990 levels). A system of carbon trading for power stations, energy-intensive companies and, at a later date, airlines, to allow them to buy or sell emission rights to third parties as required. The CO_2 emissions for new cars were immediately subject to tougher limits;

- An increase in the share of total energy output provided by renewable energy (wind, solar and biomass) to 20 percent by 2020, with binding targets set for each country;[144]
- A 20 percent cut in overall energy consumption, to be achieved by measures such as improved insulation in homes and factories.

This package of measures was not drawn up by the Commission president Barroso, but by the Belgian Jos Delbeke. An economist by training, Delbeke was promoted to director-general in the climate action department, which was set up when the new Commission took office. He came up with the idea of assigning a market value to emission rights, so that companies would have an incentive to cut emissions.

This legislation, known as the 20/20/20 plan, entered into force in June 2009. But problems are already looming. The member states' enthusiasm for sticking to the agreement has waned significantly with the onset of the financial crisis. It cooled even further during the Copenhagen Summit in December 2009 as it became increasingly clear that China was not prepared to enter into any binding agreements on a percentage cut in its CO_2 emissions.[145] In fact, Europe stood alone in its approach to climate change.

The only result to emerge from Copenhagen was a declaration that global temperatures must not be allowed to rise by more than two degrees. This was a decision reached jointly by President Obama along with China, Brazil and South Africa – but without any input from the EU. It now falls to the teams of Hedegaard and Delbeke to find a way forward, but it certainly isn't going to be easy.

144 Under the agreement, the UK is committed to increasing the share of renewables from the current 1.3% to 15%, Ireland from 3.1% to 16%, Germany from 5.8% to 18% and France from 10.33% to 23%.

145 This does not mean that China is not taking climate change seriously. The country has invested enormously in research into new energy technology and is now world leader in the solar energy and wind energy sectors.

Photo:
José Manuel Barroso at a press conference on climate change

47

19 November 2009
Finally, the European Council has a permanent president

'I have never chosen. Normally you are chosen.'[146] On 25 January 1999, Herman Van Rompuy wrote those words in his diary. Eleven years later, the Belgian prime minister stood up in his home town of Brussels and made the following statement to the world press:

'Even if it is particularly difficult to abandon the leadership of my country, I accept your decision and would like to thank you for this honour. I take it as a mark of recognition towards Belgium, which, as a founding State, has dedicated itself constantly to the construction of Europe. I have not sought this high position. I have intervened in no way. But from tonight, I will take it up with conviction.'[147]

On 19 November 2009, Van Rompuy was appointed by his fellow heads of state and government as the first permanent president of the European Council. He had to get used to all the international attention. In fact, he hadn't wanted the job.

'Up until the last moment, I did everything I could to refuse the appointment. The Swedish prime minister Reinfeldt, who served as rotating president of the EU in the second half of 2009, will remember this. 'Strike me off the list,' I told him when a consensus had been formed around my name. 'I am not a candidate'. It was pointless. Two days later, the pressure was so great that I could no longer refuse.'[148]

It seemed a strange choice. When the European Council was created in 1974, Belgium was opposed to the new body (as were Luxembourg and the Netherlands). So how could a Belgian land the plum job of first permanent president? The answer is that an agreement was reached among Europe's largest countries (Germany, France and the UK) and the two main political families (christian democrats and socialists). Initially, it looked as if Tony Blair (one of the godfathers of the new EU role) had the best chance of getting the job. But there was a danger that he would hog the limelight. He had also blotted his copybook (especially with Angela Merkel) for joining Bush in invading Iraq.

146 Herman Van Rompuy, *De binnenkant op een kier*, 2000, p. 69.

147 Herman Van Rompuy, speech of 19 November 2009.

148 Herman van Rompuy, quoted in *Pèlerin*, 6 May 2010.

112

Merkel didn't push for a German candidate. It was more important in her eyes to get a German appointed to head the European Central Bank in Frankfurt. She in fact liked the discreet style of Van Rompuy, who as prime minister of Belgium had brought calm to a troubled nation. President Sarkozy also backed Van Rompuy because he spoke good French[149] and had dealt efficiently with the banking crisis that had engulfed Dexia and Fortis.

The British prime minister, Gordon Brown, continued to support Tony Blair. He didn't succeed, but his stand led to a British person getting the second most important job created by the Lisbon Treaty – European Union High Representative for Foreign Affairs and Security Policy. The post went to Catherine Ashton, who met all the requirements. She was the right political colour (socialist), the right sex (female) and the right nationality to appease Gordon Brown. The only problem was that she had no experience of foreign affairs.

149 Balkenende of the Netherlands didn't speak French, which weakened his hand. Sarkozy was also keen to ensure that Michel Barnier was given the internal market fortfolio in the new Commission.

She also had no idea that she would be offered the job. At the time, she worked in Brussels as EU Commissioner for Trade. When she received a phone call telling her to come quickly to Schuman, she was apparently on her way home.

When the press gathered on that November evening in Brussels to find out who had been appointed to the new EU posts, they were understandably surprised at the outcome. The two figures were virtually unknown outside EU circles. In his opening address, Van Rompuy spoke quietly.

...

Photo:
Herman van Rompuy at the Brussels Summit on 19 November 2009

'We are living through exceptionally difficult times: the financial crisis and its dramatic impact on employment and budgets, the climate crisis which threatens our very survival. A period of anxiety, uncertainty and lack of confidence. Yet these problems can be overcome by common efforts in and between our countries. [...]

Our Union belongs to every one of us, we are not playing a zero-sum game. Europe must be in every member state's advantage. This cardinal principle leads me to a two-track approach. First of all, I will consider everyone's interests and sensitivities. Even if our unity is our strength, our diversity remains our wealth. Every country has its own history, its own culture, its own way of doing things. Our journey may be towards a common destination, but we will all bring along different luggage. Denying this would be counterproductive.

Without respect for our diversity, we will never build our unity. I will always bear this principle in mind. Logically, this principle has a consequence for our actions: as far as I am concerned, every country should emerge victorious from negotiations. A negotiation that ends with a defeated party is never a good negotiation. As President of the Council I will listen carefully to everyone and I will make sure that our deliberations turn into results for everyone. [...]

My whole political life has been marked by a search for understanding, respecting both adversaries and travel companions. I shall continue along this same path.' [150]

150 Herman Van Rompuy, speech of 19 November 2009.

Meanwhile, the socialist George Papandréou had been elected prime minister of Greece. In early 2010, he would reveal that the Greek deficit was far greater than the previous government had admitted, leading to one of the biggest rifts in the history of Europe.

10 February 2010
Barroso Commission II takes over

On 10 February 2010, a new team of European Commissioners arrived in Brussels, led once again by the Portuguese José Manuel Barroso. The Commissioners – eighteen men and nine women – were put forward by the 27 member states and then subjected to a tough series of individual hearings in the European Parliament. It was only once they had passed this hurdle that they were they considered fit to initiate and implement legislation and act on behalf of the European Union until the end of 2014.[151] The Commissioners meet every Wednesday on the 13th floor of the Berlaymont building in Brussels to draft European laws that will have a profound effect on the lives of some 500 million EU citizens. It's important, therefore, to know who these people are and what drives their decisions.

- José Manuel Barroso (Portuguese), president of the Commission, often seen in news broadcasts standing next to the permanent president Herman Van Rompuy. Despite the physical proximity, Barroso is keen to prevent the European Council from interfering in economic issues, which have traditionally been the responsibility of the Commission. Johannes Laitenberger, a German lawyer who speaks fluent Portuguese, is currently Barroso's chef de cabinet.

- Catherine Ashton (British), foreign and security policy. When this function was being conceived, it was seen by one senior official as 'the sexiest innovation of the Lisbon Treaty'.[152] Catherine Ashton is not only vice-president of the Commission; she also represents the EU abroad and chairs the monthly Council meetings of foreign ministers. But many critics are sceptical about her ability to perform these different roles. Her success very much depends on member states agreeing on common lines on foreign policy issues, and on the functioning of the External Action Service, set up on January 1, 2011.[153]

- Michel Barnier (French), internal market and services. Barnier knows a great deal about Europe's legislative machinery (he was a member of

151 The number of Commissioners is currently set at one per member state but, as of 2014, the figure will be adjusted to represent two-thirds of the total number of member states. As a result, the Commission, which is required to act in the interests of Europe, will become less likely to bend to pressure from individual member states.

152 'Too many cooks', in *The Economist*, 17 December 2009.

153 To create the External Action Service, the Directorate-General (DG) External Relations and parts of DG Development (as well as the 136 overseas delegations they supervised), were stripped from the Commission and combined with Council Secretariat officials and diplomats from the national member states. See http://eeas.europa.eu for more information.

the Prodi Commission (1999-2004) with responsibility for institutional reform, worked as a French minister on the Amsterdam Treaty and also played a role in the Convention). He is now in charge of developing a mechanism to supervise and regulate the financial sector – a project that emerged, at least partly, following the eurozone crisis of 2010.

· Olli Rehn (Finnish), economic and monetary affairs. Rehn, 47, enjoys playing rugby in his free time. Would the techniques that he employs on the rugby pitch help him to implement the far-reaching legislative package designed to strengthen European economic governance? Under these proposed laws, member states are required to submit their budgets and reform plans every year to the Commission, which will submit them to peer review even before the policies are voted on by the national parliaments (the so-called European Semester). Countries will not only be monitored for excessive deficits and debts, but also for macro-economic imbalances and falling competitiveness. Financial sanctions for euro-area member states will kick in earlier, on more grounds, and decisions will be reached more easily than in the past.[154] With these measures, says the Commission, economic and monetary union will finally stand on its two feet.

154 A Commission proposal for imposing a fine will be considered adopted unless turned down by the Council via qualified majority.

We have already discussed the Commissioners Karel De Gucht (Belgian, trade), Neelie Kroes (Netherlands, digital agenda), Joaquin Almunia (Spanish, competition), Stefan Füle (Czech, EU enlargement) and Connie Hedegaard (Danish, climate action). The other Commissioners in Barroso's team

Photo:
Group photograph of all 27 Commissioners appointed to the Barroso II Commission

are: László Andor (Hungarian, employment and social affairs), Dacian Cio-los (Romanian, agriculture and rural development), John Dalli (Maltese, health and consumer affairs), Maria Damanaki (Greek, fisheries), Máire Geoghegan-Quinn (Irish, research and innovation), Kristalina Georgieva (Bulgarian, humanitarian aid and crisis response), Johannes Hahn (Austrian, regional policy), Siim Kallas (Estonian, transport), Janusz Lewandowski (Polish, budget), Cecilia Malmström (Swedish, home affairs), Günther Oettinger (German, energy), Andris Piebalgs (Latvian, development), Janez Potocnik (Slovenian, environment), Viviane Reding (Luxembourgish, justice, fundamental rights and citizenship), Maros Sefcovic (Slovakian, institutional policy), Algirdas Semeta (Lithuanian, taxation and customs union, audit and anti-fraud), Antonio Tajani (Italian, industry and entrepreneurship), Androulla Vassiliou (Cypriot, education, culture, multilingualism and youth). This official photograph shows all of the Commissioners ready to take on their new responsibilities in 2010.

6 May 2010
The European Parliament shows its teeth

Majestic buildings clad with dazzling glass. Marble-lined lobbies, countless escalators and lifts. Doors that suddenly open to reveal unexpected wings. Members of parliament hurrying along long corridors on their way from one committee meeting to another (European legislative proposals are discussed in specialised parliamentary committees). Bars where members drink Italian espresso, forge political alliances and agree on compromises. The European debating chamber, presided over by the Polish Jerzy Buzek, where the 736 MEPs meet to vote or to listen to someone who has a message to deliver.

External speakers are regularly invited to address the European Parliament. On 6 May 2010, one such speaker was Joe Biden, Vice President of the United States. One month before, on 11 April, the eurozone finance ministers had approved a €30 billion rescue plan for Greece, which was on the verge of bankruptcy due to a colossal government deficit representing 13.6 percent of GDP. This had had been covered up for many years, but now the Greek government was no longer in a position to support the debt burden.

155 Remarks by Vice President Biden to the European Parliament, 6 May 2010, The White House.

The bailout failed to reassure nervous financial markets. On 2 May 2010, after days of foot-dragging by the German Chancellor Angela Merkel, an emergency plan was drawn up involving a cash injection to the tune of €110 billion combined with a ruthless cost-cutting plan that the International Monetary Fund (IMF) would help to monitor. The financial markets were now asking the question: what if the financial crisis spreads to Portugal and Spain? Investors became nervous. Bank shares plummeted. Relations between countries that shared the euro became overheated. Was this the end of the European single currency? This issue was in the news when Joe Biden, President Obama's right-hand man, stood up in the European Parliament to deliver his speech. 'Last year,' he began, 'the United States and Europe acted quickly and decisively when the world was reeling from a financial crisis that was more profound than any since the Great Depression. And in doing so, collectively we helped prevent what people were predicting, the total collapse of the world economy. And today, President Obama and I are closely following the economic and financial crisis in Greece and the European Union's efforts to deal with it. We welcome the support package that Europe is considering, in conjunction the International Monetary Fund. And we will be supportive both directly and through the IMF of your efforts as you rescue Greece.'[155]

Biden also wanted to raise an issue that had for some time now been souring relations between Europe and the United States: did the US authorities still have an unlimited right to snoop into European bank accounts in order to track down planned terrorist acts and prevent them occurring?[156] The European member states said they did – in November 2009, they concluded a provisional agreement that permitted the bulk transfer of bank data. But the European Parliament argued that this failed to safeguard sufficiently the European citizen's right to privacy. Moreover, the opinion of MEPs had suddenly become much more important, following the implementation of the Lisbon Treaty which granted them far greater powers. International agreements, for example, could now only be concluded after they had been approved by the European Parliament (Lisbon Treaty, art. 218). The European Parliament immediately seized on this new right, following the recommendation of a Dutch rapporteur on the issue of banking data. She advised them to vote against, which they did in February 2010.[157] As a result, the agreement with the United States was effectively blocked, leading to enormous relief among the MEPs and shock and disbelief within the White House.

Biden was no doubt thinking of this decision when he spoke in the European Parliament. 'President Obama has said that keeping our country safe is the first thing he thinks about when he wakes up in the morning and the last

...

156 SWIFT, the company responsible for managing the confidential banking data, was based in Belgium, so the US authorities needed the EU authorities to approve the data transfer.

157 In every case involving proposed legislation or a treaty under negotiation, a member of parliament is appointed as 'rapporteur'. This person, who is responsible for writing a report, plays a crucial role in the position adopted by the European Parliament. In her report on the SWIFT agreement regarding the transfer of EU banking data to the US, the rapporteur was the young Dutch politician Jeanine Hennis-Plasschaert of the liberal VVD party. She recommended to her colleagues that they reject the agreement, which led to a standing ovation in the parliament. She was voted MEP of the Year in 2010 by the European Voice.

Photo:
Joe Biden, Vice President of the United States (left) with Jerzy Buzek, President of the European Parliament, at the European Parliament in Brussels

158 Remarks by Vice
President Biden
to the European
Parliament, 6 May
2010, The White
House.

159 Germany, with its
99 representatives,
has the largest
number of MEPs,
followed by Britain,
France and Italy
with 72 elected rep-
resentatives each.
See *www.europarl.
europa/members*
for detailed infor-
mation.

thing he thinks about before he goes to bed at night,' he told MEPs. 'I suspect that is how every world leader looks at their role. Indeed, no less than privacy, physical safety is also an inalienable right. [...] We understand your concerns. As a consequence, we are working together to address them and I'm absolu- tely confident that we can succeed, to both use the tool and guarantee privacy. It's important that we do so, and it's important that we do so as quickly as possible.[...].' [158]

The MEPs present in the chamber applauded politely at the end the speech. After the applause died away, Joe Biden (who had been a senator himself for the past 36 years) was surrounded by security guards and led to the exit.

Biden's visit was proof of the newly-acquired status of the European Par- liament in the eyes of the world. More than ever, it was now important for world leaders (and others) to know who had been elected to sit for five years in the European Parliament and what exactly they were doing. [159]

9 May 2010

The eurozone receives
a massive bailout

On Sunday 9 May 2010, sixty years to the day after Robert Schuman launched the plan in Paris that started everything off, the European Union arrived at a crucial turning point. The Greek debt crisis had spread to Ireland, Portugal, Spain and beyond. Dominique Strauss-Kahn, head of the International Monetary Fund (IMF), and Jean-Claude Trichet, head of the European Central Bank (ECB), managed to convince German Chancellor Angela Merkel that the fate of the euro was hanging by a thread. President Obama took up the telephone and made a long call to Merkel, Sarkozy and Zapatero. Meanwhile, in Brussels, Europe's finance ministers worked throughout the day and long into the night alongside representatives of the IMF and the ECB in a desperate bid to find a solution to the crisis.[160]

At two o'clock in the morning, just before the Asian markets opened for trading, the Spanish finance minister announced a temporary plan (up to 2013) for a massive bailout. It contained four major components.

- The European Commission could lend up to €60 billion to eurozone countries experiencing difficulties under a so-called European Financial Stabilisation Mechanism (EFSM), guaranteed by the EU's budget.
- The eurozone countries pledged €440 billion in guarantees to provide loans to countries in trouble. In order to raise the necessary capital, the EU set up a special-purpose vehicle known as the European Financial Stability Facility (EFSF), which took the form of a limited liability company.[161] The Commission had control over the facility, but member states decided individually whether they would provide guarantees to countries in trouble that came knocking at its door.
- The IMF offered to contribute €250 billion.
- The ECB could buy up government bonds and company stocks on the financial markets to ensure liquidity in markets that were in trouble. This meant that the ECB, which had been set up to avoid inflation in the eurozone, was entering unchartered territory. This decision was far from popular, in particular with the Germans – who are still haunted by memories of the hyperinflation that rocked the economy in 1922-23.

160 Wolfgang Schäuble, the German finance minister, became ill during the marathon meeting and ended up in a Brussels hospital. He was replaced by Thomas de Maizière, Germany's interior minister.

161 The EFSF is based in Luxemburg and headed by the German Klaus Regling, who played a key role in drawing up the Stability and Growth Pact in the late 1990s.

German Chancellor Angela Merkel, who played a key role in this episode, appeared to have caved in to French and American pressure. But her steadfast demeanour showed that she was determined to do everything in her power to ensure that countries that failed to control their budget and national debt would be forced to take measures to correct the problem. The coming years will be marked by strict spending controls.

'This is more than just a crisis,' she said a few days later. 'Europe is facing the biggest challenge since the fall of Communism. [...] The challenge is existential, and has to be met. If it fails, the consequences for Europe and the rest of the world are impossible to imagine. But if it succeeds, then Europe will emerge stronger than ever before.'[162]

162 Angela Merkel, Speech in Aachen, 13 May 2010.

The permanent president of the European Council, Herman van Rompuy, was only partially involved in these crucial negotiations. But he had a clear message to deliver to the people of Europe on the occasion of the 60th anniversary of the Schuman Declaration.

'We do not ask for enthusiasm and European flag waving, we do not ask you to join a chorus for peace. We just ask for your awareness. We should like you to be aware that when we negotiate a deal or solve the crisis of the day, there often is more at stake than just the deal, more than just the crisis. At the height of those moments, the fate of Europe itself is often in the balance. Together, we defend a treasure that is dear to us.

Photo:
Angela Merkel at the start of a meeting in Berlin on 6 May 2010 to discuss a financial bailout for the ailing Greek economy

Let me remind you what we defend. Europeans have a privileged place in the world. Our countries are envied for their political stability, for their welfare and their social systems, for the quality of European life. You, the half a billion men and women who live in the European Union, are amongst the most educated and trained people in the world. We are the world's largest power in trade. These are accomplishments to be proud of. [...]'

'However,' he continued, 'in a world of change, other regions are ready to out-perform us economically. Our jobs and our influence are at stake. [...] Today's world requires us notably to develop a stronger economic policy and more united foreign and climate policies. I am glad that all members of the European Council are ready to assume this common responsibility.'

'Sixty years ago,' Van Rompuy concluded, 'Schuman and the others embarked on a common venture. The countries that joined it have fared well. It is no longer confined to 'Brussels'. It is about the prosperity, security and common destiny of 500 million people living in 27 democracies on our beautiful continent. Today, I ask you only one thing, to pause a moment and to realise: We, Europeans, are in this together.'[163]

Twelve month and two rescue packages later (€85 billion for Ireland and €78 billion for Portugal), a rumour in early May 2011 that Greece was considering an exit from the eurozone proved that the euro crisis was far from over.

Prodded by Angela Merkel, EU member states have agreed on an amendment to the Lisbon Treaty setting up a permanent successor to the temporary facility: the European Stability Mechanism (ESM).[164] The Stability Mechanism, due to replace the EFSF in 2013, will have an effective lending capacity of €500 billion ensured by guarantees and paid-in capital. In addition, 23 member states are committed to coordinating their economic policy reforms (wages, labour markets and pensions) beyond existing rules under a 'Euro-Plus' Pact. (The United Kingdom, Sweden, Hungary and the Czech Republic have opted out).

These decisions have helped to avert a European crisis in the short term. The longer-term survival of the euro in its current form, however, is not yet guaranteed.

163 Herman Van Rompuy, 'Europe Needs You Today', article published in several European newspapers on the 60th anniversary of the Schuman Declaration, 9 May, 2010.

164 'The Member States whose currency is the euro may establish a stability mechanism to be activated if indispensable to safeguard the stability of the euro area as a whole. The granting of any required financial assistance under the mechanism will be made subject to strict conditionality.' Such is the legal language added to article 136 of the Lisbon Treaty, under a new and simplified procedure.

Index

A

Adenauer, Konrad, 13, 15, 21, 22, 29, 59, 65, 103
Almunia, Joaquin, 107, 116
Amato, Giuliano, 87, 89, 91
Amsterdam, Treaty of, 80-82, 116
Andreotti, Giulio, 52, 54, 64
Ashton, Catherine, 39, 88, 109, 113, 115
Attlee, Clement, 14
Aznar, José María, 80-81, 88, 94

B

Balkenende, Jan-Peter, 88, 100, 104, 113
Balmer, Steve, 105,
Barnier, Michel, 113, 115
Barroso, José Manuel, 39, 88, 95, 98, 103, 108, 110-111, 115-116
Bech, Joseph, 15, 21
Berlusconi, Silvio, 95, 99
Biden, Joe, 118-120
Bolkestein, Frits, 84, 96-98
Blair, Tony, 69, 80, 86, 88, 94-95, 99, 100, 103, 108, 112
Brandt, Willy, 33, 36, 38, 40
Brittan, Leon, 20, 75
Brown, Gordon, 108, 113

C

Chirac, Jacques, 80, 84, 88, 95, 99-100
Cockfield, Arthur, 49, 50-51
Copenhagen criteria, 72-73, 101
Couve de Murville, Maurice, 29-30
Craxi, Bettino, 46, 52-53

D

Dankert, Piet, 68
De Boissieu, Pierre, 67
De Clercq, Willy, 48-49, 74
De Gaulle, Charles, 24-26, 29-30, 31-32, 34, 35, 42, 67
De Gucht, Karel, 20, 74-75, 116
Dehaene, Jean-Luc, 77, 81-82, 87, 89, 91
De Jong, Piet, 33
Delbeke, Jos, 111
Delors, Jacques, 19, 32, 43, 47, 48-49, 50-51, 52, 54, 55, 56-57, 59-60, 62, 64, 67, 68, 72-73, 74-75, 76-77, 78, 94, 96
Den Uyl, Joop, 40-41
Dooge, James, 47, 52
Donner, André, 27

E

ECB (European Central Bank), 56-57, 76, 83, 113, 121
ECSC (European Coal and Steel Community), 14-15, 16, 18
EEC (European Economic Community), 20-21, 22-23, 24-26, 29-30, 31-32, 33-34, 35-36, 37, 40, 42, 44-45, 46, 50, 52, 59, 62, 63, 66
EEA (European Economic Area), 78-79
EFTA (European Free Trade Association), 24-25, 35-36, 78-79
Eisenhower, Dwight, 16
EMS (European Monetary System), 43, 56-57
Eppink, Derk-Jan, 94, 97-98, 120
Erhard, Ludwig, 29-30
Euratom, 20-21
European Defence Community, 16-17

European constitution, 86, 87-88, 89-91, 98, 99-100, 101, 103, 108-109
Eyskens, Gaston, 33
Eyskens, Mark, 68

F

Fitzgerald, Garret, 46, 52
Fontainebleau Agreement, 46-47
Füle, Stefan, 101, 116

G

Garton Ash, Timothy, 66, 80, 84
Giscard d'Estaing, Valéry, 40-41, 42-43, 44-45, 56, 87-88, 89-91
Gonzalez, Felipe, 64
Gorbachev, Mikhail, 58-60, 61-62, 63, 65, 77
Gore, Al, 110

H

Havel, Vaclav, 58, 65, 92
Hallstein, Walter, 21, 22, 28, 29-30, 32
Heath, Edward, 25, 35
Hedegaard, Connie, 110-111
High Authority, 12, 14, 16-17, 20
Honecker, Erich, 58-59

I

IMF (International Monetary Fund), 118-119

K

Kantor, Mickey, 75
Kaczynski, Lech, 103
Kennedy, John F., 25
Kennedy Round, 74
Kissinger Henry, 37-39

Kohl, Helmut, 46-47, 52, 54, 56-57, 59, 62, 63-64, 65-66, 70, 76-77, 80, 84
Kok, Wim, 80
Kohnstamm, Max, 14, 16-17
Kroes, Neelie, 20, 105-107, 116

L
Laeken Declaration, 85-86, 87
Lamy, Pascal, 48-49, 50, 75
Lisbon, Treaty of, 41, 69, 82, 87-88, 90, 93, 100-101, 103-104, 108-109, 113, 115, 119, 123
Lubbers, Ruud, 46, 52, 63-64, 65, 69-70, 76-77
Luns, Joseph, 21, 24, 30-31
Luxembourg Compromise, 31-32, 55, 74

M
Macmillan, Harold, 24-26
Major, John, 66, 69, 77
Maastricht, Treaty of, 57, 67-68, 69-71, 72, 78, 80
Mansholt, Sicco, 22-23
Martens, Wilfried, 46, 52, 64,
McCreevy, Charles, 98
Merkel, Angela, 66, 95, 102, 103-104, 112-113, 118, 121-123
Mitterrand, François, 46, 52, 62, 63-64, 65-66, 77, 84
Monnet, Jean, 13, 14, 16-17, 18, 40, 48, 100
Monti, Mario, 105

N
NATO, 16-17, 25, 65, 95
Nixon, Richard, 37-38

O
Obama, Barack, 39, 109, 111, 118, 119, 121

P
Papandréou, Andreas, 46, 52-53
Papandréou, George, 114
Paris, Treaty of, 14-15, 16, 27
Pineau, Christian, 21
Pleven, René, 16-17
Pöhl, Karl Otto, 57
Pompidou, Georges, 33-34, 36, 40, 42
Prodi, Romano, 94, 116

R
Reagan, Ronald, 61
Rehn, Olli, 116
Rey, Jean, 32
Rome, Treaty of, 20-21, 22, 27-28, 30, 42, 59, 50, 52-53, 54, 60, 99, 108

S
Santer, Jacques, 52, 64, 77
Sarkozy, Nicolas, 102, 103, 106-107, 113, 121
Schabowski, Günter, 61
Schengen Agreement, 79, 81
Schlüter, Poul 46, 52-53
Schmidt, Helmut, 40-41, 43, 44-45
Schröder, Gerhard, 80, 84, 88, 93, 94-95
Schuman, Robert, 12-13, 14-15, 16-17, 86, 100, 113, 121-123
Segni, Antonio, 21
Single European Act, 54-55
Sforza, Carlo, 15
Spaak, Paul-Henri, 17, 18-19, 20-21, 24, 30-31, 47, 60

Stability and Growth Pact, 83-84, 121
Stikker, Dirk, 15
Strauss-Kahn, Dominique, 121

T
Tindemans, Leo, 40-41, 55
Thatcher, Margaret, 44-45, 46, 50, 52-53, 56-57, 60, 62, 63-64, 65-66, 100
Thorn, Gaston, 41, 46
Trichet, Jean-Claude, 121

U
Uruguay Round, 74-75

V
Van den Broek, Hans, 68
Van Gend & Loos decision, 27-28
Van Middelaar, Luuk, 53, 64, 66, 68, 88
Van Miert, Karel, 20
Van Rompuy, Herman, 39, 68, 88, 108-109, 112-114, 115, 123
Van Zeeland, Paul, 15
Veil, Simone, 43
Verhofstadt, Guy, 41, 85-86, 94-95, 104

W
Walesa, Lech, 58
Werner, Pierre, 33, 46, 61

Z
Zapatero, José Luis Rodriguez, 103, 109, 121

Hanneke Siebelink has always been intrigued by the stories that lie behind European cooperation. Born in Brussels, she studied at Leuven University where she gained a degree in applied economics. She went on to study the Italian language in Perugia, after which she obtained a Masters in European Studies at the London School of Economics. She then worked in Brussels for ten years as an adviser to the US Mission to the European Union, where she gained a deep understanding of both EU and US policy.

Siebelink currently lives in Brussels with her husband and two sons. She enjoys meeting people and finding out what drives them, but tries to avoid logging onto her Twitter account before she has eaten breakfast.

While working on this book, Siebelink travelled extensively in Central Europe. She has previously published a book in Dutch, *Abraham Lincoln, Over Mezelf* (*Abraham Lincoln, About Myself*), and recently started working on a new book about China.

Credits

The 50 Days that Changed Europe

Author: Hanneke Siebelink
Translation: Derek Blyth
Photo editor: Karoline Neujens
Graphic Design: Joke Gossé

Cover image: © Belga (East Side Gallery, Berlin)
Photo Credits: pp. 21, 23, 43, 45, 47, 64, 73, 75,
77, 79, 104, 109, 111, 116 (European Commission)
pp. 13, 15, 19, 25, 30, 34, 38, 41, 49, 51, 53, 55,
59, 62, 66, 70, 81, 90, 95, 97, 100, 106, 113, 119,
122 (Belga)

Typefaces: National and Melville
Printed in Belgium by Proost nv on
Muncken Print Cream

D/2011/12.005/14
ISBN 978 94 6058 0796
NUR 697

© 2011 Luster, Belgium
info@lusterweb.com